Kitchen Dynamics

THE RICE WAY

Books in the ABICS Publications Series

Badiru, Deji, **Kitchen Dynamics: The Rice Way**, iUniverse, Bloomington, Indiana, USA, 2016

Badiru, Deji, **Consumer Economics: Time Value of Dollars and Sense,** iUniverse, Bloomington, Indiana, USA, 2015

Badiru, Deji, **Youth Soccer Training Slides: A Math and Science Approach,** iUniverse, Bloomington, Indiana, USA, 2014

Badiru, Deji, **My Little Blue Book of Project Management: What, When, Who, and How,** iUniverse, Bloomington, Indiana, USA, 2014

Badiru, Deji, **8 by 3 Model of Time Management: Balancing Work, Home, and Leisure,** iUniverse, Bloomington, Indiana, USA, 2013

Badiru, Deji, **Badiru's Equation of Success: Intelligence, Common Sense, and Self-discipline,** iUniverse, Bloomington, Indiana, USA, 2013

Badiru, Deji, **Blessings of a Father: Education Contributions of Father Slattery at Saint Finbarr's College,** Bloomington, Indiana, USA, 2013

Badiru, Iswat and Deji Badiru, **Isi Cookbook: Collection of Easy Nigerian Recipes,** iUniverse, Bloomington, Indiana, USA, 2013

Badiru, Deji and Iswat Badiru, **Physics in the Nigerian Kitchen: The Science, the Art, and the Recipes,** iUniverse, Bloomington, Indiana, USA, 2013.

Badiru, Deji, **Physics of Soccer: Using Math and Science to Improve Your Game,** iUniverse, Bloomington, Indiana, USA, 2010.

Badiru, Deji, **Getting things done through project management,** iUniverse, Bloomington, Indiana, USA, 2009.

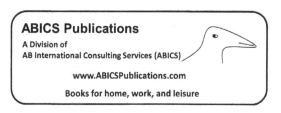

ABICS Publications
A Division of
AB International Consulting Services (ABICS)

www.ABICSPublications.com
Books for home, work, and leisure

Kitchen Dynamics

THE RICE WAY

DEJI BADIRU

KITCHEN DYNAMICS
THE RICE WAY

iUniverse books may be ordered through booksellers or by contacting:

iUniverse
1663 Liberty Drive
Bloomington, IN 47403
www.iuniverse.com
1-800-Authors (1-800-288-4677)

ISBN: 978-1-4917-8899-8 (sc)
ISBN: 978-1-4917-8898-1 (e)

Print information available on the last page.

iUniverse rev. date: 02/12/2016

Contents

Dedication

To rice aficionados, who stretch the conventional
boundaries of cooking and eating rice

Acknowledgments

I gratefully acknowledge the versatility of rice to sustain life in all corners of the World.

I thank all the friends, family, and colleagues, who provided personal favorite rice recipes for this book. Great thanks go to my partner of 40+ years, Iswat, whose kitchen experiments generated several of the recipes adapted from her Isi Cookbook. Special thanks also go to Maria Miah, Elsa Swire, Ginger Swire-Clark, Deb Donley, Penny Davis, and John Colombi, who generously contributed recipes to enhance the culinary diversity of Kitchen Dynamics: The Rice Way. Bon Appetit to all.

Synopsis

Kitchen Dynamics: The Rice Way is a delightful and humorous rendition of my love of the most popular food in the world, rice. In addition to rice recipes, the book discusses the efficacy of rice in the ethnic diet. As a rice purist, I prefer unadulterated steamed white rice. The other types of cooked rice, such as friend rice, yellow rice, and jollof rice are just a matter of seasoning and garnishing. Although I have harbored the desire to write this book for many years, a December 2015 visit to Hawaii provided the final impetus to go ahead and write the book now. The contents of this book contain technical facts, cultural tales, worldwide appreciation, and recipes of rice. My poetic ode to rice is presented in the first chapter. Nothing beats the sight of a ladle in a pot of rice and beans. So, this book also contains rice-complementing recipes that casual observers might not recognize as excellent accompaniments for rice. A distended stomach that is pumped full of rice is a good remedy for hunger. This speaks well of the versatility of rice in our collective efforts of sustaining life. Readers are welcome to read and enjoy the contents of *"Kitchen Dynamics: The Rice Way"* and are encouraged to experiment with cooking and eating rice in all its culinary ramifications.

Chapter 1

The Rice of My Soul

"Rice time is good time; good time is rice time."
– Deji Badiru

Food is a universal language that we all speak and understand very well. Food is central to life and life revolves around food. Those who have a passion for life also have a passion for food. So, food and life are inseparable. As a result, we should recognize and worship the central role of food in our lives. Rice, as a basic food item in all cultures, deserves a special treatment. Rice is central to all our food cultures. In many countries, rice is the difference between life and death. It is the staple food. The special treatment of rice is exactly what "Kitchen Dynamics: The Rice Way" presents.

I offer some words of explanation, definition, and clarification of my choice of this book's title. In scientific terms, *dynamics* is the branch of mechanics concerned with the motion of bodies under the action of forces. In organizational terms, dynamics refers to how the elements (people and resources) within an organization behave, act, and react to each other for the purpose of moving the organization forward efficiently and effectively. In terms of the title of this book, dynamics refers to how the subsystems (people, ingredients, tools, and equipment) within an overall kitchen system act and coordinate together to produce desired culinary outputs. Rice plays a central role in kitchen dynamics.

Rice is an edible starchy cereal grain. Rice makes every soul rise. Rice translates to relief for hunger and starvation. There is always a lot of drama surrounding the presence of rice on the dinner table, or the breakfast and lunch tables, for that matter. A breakfast rice experience at a Michigan hotel in 2014 added to the several long-held reasons for writing this book. I was at an upscale hotel in the Detroit, Michigan area, where I noticed that rice was served for breakfast along with the conventional continental breakfast items at most Western Hotels. In my world travels, the sight of rice at breakfast is a common expectation. I have had rice for breakfast in Lagos (Nigeria), Seoul (South Korea), Dubai (United Arab Emirates), Singapore, Kuwait, Cancun (Mexico), as well as many other popular world locations. But steamed rice for breakfast at an upscale US hotel was a first for me, despite my over four decades of food-foraging around the USA. I was delightfully surprised. It was a tantalizing offer. This was not an expected prospect on the continental breakfast line. So, while scooping up a hearty portion of the rice from the table-top rice cooker, I posed a question to the attendant, "I am glad to see rice among the breakfast offering, but this is the first time I am seeing rice offered for breakfast at a USA hotel. Why?" I asked. I went on to quip, "Are we internationalizing USA hotels?" She gracefully responded, "This being the auto industry area, we host many Asian guests and they demand rice as one of the food options for breakfast." I thought to myself, Yea! Those are my people, the rice people! The word "demand" resonates well with me in this regard, rather than "request." Rice is the epitome of intermingling of food, geography, and socio-economic politics. You will find an endless talk of rice in Malay, Chinese, Indian, Boneo, Brunei, Nepalese, and African socio-economic discourse. In many ethnic grocery stores around the world, rice represents a colorful tapestry of grains.

In my mind, rice is what is needed to get the soul soaring early in the morning. The soul rises with every speck of rice it can muster. So it goes that I am closing this opening chapter with my own ode to rice.

==============================

Deji's Ode to Rice

Rice, in my hot water, you rise magically.
You are the rice of my soul.
You are the rise of my day.
You are the apple of my eye.
When I see you, I salivate.
I live for you, you grow for me.
What a nice partnership that is!
You make me rise every morning;
You are the springboard of my day;
Each day, I rise to relish my rice;
The anchor of my recipe;
The root of my existence;
Without you, I am nothing but jelly;
I dream of you when I miss you on my plate;
Yes, you are my soul mate;
You are the very rice of my soul.
May you always rest in perfect harmony with my plate!

© 2014 Adedeji Badiru, ABICS Publications

==============================

Food origin is the very origin of Mankind. Biology determines what we are. Chemistry explains what makes us what we are. Physics describes what we do. Food is an essential dimension of our existence.

The statement above is a manifestation of the biology, chemistry, and physics engendered in all manners of food preparation over the millennia. The history of food preparation goes back to the very beginning of man and woman. Since the dawn of time, human beings have taken delight in the science and art of cooking and eating. Culinary expertise and gastronomic interests are continually combined to satisfy our ever increasingly sophisticated palate. We tickle our palate with new food experiences and experimentations. A person's food preferences are shaped by several factors including the following:

- Country of origin
- Personal health consciousness
- Religion
- Economic order
- Cultural affiliation
- Ethnic origin
- Social class
- Language cluster

- Family group
- Community setting
- Residential locality
- Caste system
- Professional genre
- Educational awareness
- Acquired taste due to repeated trial, experimentation, or "force-feeding"

I strongly postulate that food experimentations help build a palate that tolerates different cuisines.

The Glorious Global Grace of Rice

"Rice is born in water and must die in wine." - Italian Proverb

Food, particularly rice, has played a significant role in the development of society and order of the day as evidenced by the facts below. In the early days, temples were used as banks and the first loans were taken out against rice. Where there is rice, there is less hunger. Rice, in all its glory, adorns dinner tables in all corners of the world. It is one of the most versatile and ubiquitous foods on the tables of more people around the world than any other single food item. It has, thus, been used effectively to combat hunger in impoverish parts of the world. Rice has been studied as much intellectually as it has been passed around the table. In 2005, an international news brief announced that scientists have cracked the DNA code of rice. A team of scientists from ten countries reportedly teamed up to decipher the genetic code of rice. This scientific advancement is expected to speed up attempts to improve rice as a food crop that feeds most of the world's population. Rice is the first crop plant to have its genome sequenced. This means that scientists have identified virtually all the 389 million chemical building blocks of rice's DNA. Farmers and breeders can use this information to produce new rice varieties to satisfy specific gastronomic needs. For example, higher yield, more nutritional values, and better resistance to disease and pests are possible. This will ensure that rice will continue to enjoy its royal place in kitchens around the world for generations to come. The various "seductions of rice" are profiled in the excellent book by Jeffrey Alford and Naomi Duguid entitled "Seductions of Rice: A Cookbook" (Artisan/Workman Publishing, Inc., NY, 1998).

Shizuo Tsuji Poem for Rice

"Rice is a beautiful food. It is beautiful when it grows, precision rows of sparkling green stalks shooting up to reach the hot summer sun. It is beautiful when harvested, autumn gold sheaves piled on diked, patchwork paddies. It is beautiful when, once threshed, it enters granary bins like a (flood) of tiny seed-pearls. It is beautiful when cooked by a practiced hand, pure white and sweetly fragrant." - Shizuo Tsuji

A Rice-Perfect Kitchen

Every kitchen should be rice perfect. You can have rice parfait too. One of my most-cherish kitchen gifts is a rice cookbook presented to me by my staff members at the University of Tennessee, Knoxville to on occasion of the Boss' Day in October 2004. Below is an echo of the group-signed inscription in the inside front cover of the book gift, "*Seductions of Rice*: A Cookbook" by Jeffrey Alford and Naomi Duguid (Artisan/Workman Publishing, Inc., New York, NY, 1998). The inscription conveys the message of my culinary love affair with rice. The cookbook was accompanied by a microwavable rice cooker, which is shown in the picture below.

"Happy Bosses Day – October 2004.

To: Adedeji Badiru – the best boss in the world!

From: Your staff and staff emeritus, Jeanette Myers, Christine Tidwell, Shirley McGuire, Jamie Gunter, and Ruby Tasie.
We know how much you enjoy rice! ☺*"*

Chapter 2

The Long History of Rice

Long grain rice has a long history (pun intended). The history of rice dates back to a long, long time ago. It has been reported that the consumption of rice can be traced to 2500 BC. Historical records suggest that rice production originated in China and later spread to other Asian countries, including Sri Lanka and India. It quickly spread further and has emerged as a universal food in all parts of the world. It many countries, particularly the developing countries, rice is eaten as the main course while it is eaten as a side dish or vegetable in the more advanced economies. It is suspected that rice was brought to West Asia and Greece in 300 B.C. by Alexander the Great's armies.

In the early history of trade and commerce around 800 AD, rice featured prominently in East Africa, India, and Indonesia. Nowadays, it is impossible to imagine any culture where rice is not eaten as a major contributor to subsistence. Even with its vast expanse of being geographically distant, North America did not escape from the incursion of rice. Although it is debatable how rice was first brought to North America, the fact remains that it has maintained a foothold on the continent for centuries. The arriving streams of immigrants contributed to this unmistakable presence.

One account that suggests that slaves from Africa brought rice from their lands is unfathomable to me, as an author. By and large, slaves were forcibly taken to foreign lands without an opportunity to take anything with them. They did not know where they were going and could not have planned to take any agricultural items with them. Such an act would have required advance deliberate planning. No one planned to go into slavery as a subject. Thus, this notion of slaves bringing rice grains with them is ridiculously farfetched.

It is, indeed, recorded that in 1700, 300 tons of American rice was shipped to England. This export accomplishment demonstrated the early flourishment of rice in the Americas. After the four-year American Civil War ended in 1865, rice thrived in abundant production all over the American South. Now, rice is produced consistently in commercial quantities in California, Mississippi, Texas, Arkansas, and Louisiana. Contrary to the Asian images of manually-intensive rice production, rice production in the United States has adopted new technology and machinery to facilitate large-scale production of rice. On average, it takes about seven person-hours per acre to cultivate rice. In Asia, it can take up to 300 person-hours to cultivate an acre of rice. Consumer statistics show that, on average, an American consumes around 25 pounds of rice a year. By my own household facts, that poundage of consumption is about doubled. By comparison, in parts of Asia, a consumer could down between 200 and 400 pounds of rice a year. This is a credit to the various rice-based cuisines in the Asian culture.

Rice is very adaptive and agriculturally accommodating because it can be grown in a variety of conditions, even in seemingly adverse environments. Rice can be grown in desert lands as well as in wetlands and the plant can grow to between two and six feet tall. Rice is cultivated into two separate agronomic species noted below.

- Oryza sativa
- Oryza glaberrima

Oryza sativa is much more commonly used to produce common consumption rice. Rice is grown in four different ecosystems identified below.

- Irrigated
- Rain-fed lowland
- Rain-fed upland
- Flood-prone

In terms of visibility, recognition, nutritional value, and agricultural value, rice is the most important crop in the world and the most popular food. For about 4 billion people in Asia, rice provides between 40% and 85% of their total calorie intake. Although rice provides some nutritional value, such as protein, minerals, vitamins, and fiber, it does not provide adequate nutritional value if eaten alone. However, the various ways that it is coupled with other foodstuffs in recipes makes rice acceptable as a main food source. It is known that brown rice has more nutritional value than white rice. This is because the outer brown layer of the rice contains proteins and minerals. The white part of the rice is mainly carbohydrates. One of the most admired attributes of rice is its prolonged shelf life. Rice can be stored indefinitely if it is stored in a cool and dry storage. My family and I can attest to this property of rice as we often store different varieties of rice for exceedingly long periods. Long live rice!

Chapter 3

Facts of Rice

Facts of rice are like facts of life. The science of rice goes back to ancient times. As far back as 2500 B.C. rice has been documented in the history books as a source of food and traditional celebrations. Grains of uncooked rice are thrown at many traditional weddings in many parts of the World as a sign of showering the newly wed with prosperity, fertility, and productivity.

There is a lot of fine arts and much of science pertaining to the growing, harvesting, marketing, cooking, and consuming rice. As my poem below attests, there are subtle and obvious interrelationships in human pursuits. We just have to explore and find the common basis in all we do.

===================================

**The Rhyme of Artistic Expressions:
The Arts of Cooking, Dancing, Painting, and Writing**

Behold;
The dance of meat molecules in my pot;
The dance of my pen on paper;
The dance of my paintbrush on canvas;
Oh; The tangle, twist, and tango of my feet on the dance floor;

It's all Arts to me.
Ingredients are to the recipe what paint hues are to the portrait;
Steps are to the dance what pen strokes are to the script;
And; Of course, cooking, dancing, painting, and writing are,
to me, the very existence.
Of what is life without The Arts?

Rice Facts, Properties, and Characteristics

Rice has unique properties and special characteristics. Some facts and tidbits of rice are provided below.

- The Chinese word for rice, "mi-fan," loosely translates to mean "food." Everyone loves food. So, we should all love rice.
- People often mistakenly think that rice is a Chinese food, but the fact is that rice is produced everywhere in the world, including deserts, except in Antarctica. The production is far more difficult in some regions than others. So, don't go about trying to grow rice in your backyard family garden. It only grows in aquatic conditions with a man-made paddy.
- A rice paddy is a rice field, usually kept covered with shallow water, specifically for growing rice.
- There are upland rice varieties available that can grow on dry land in warmer regions, if irrigated properly.
- Rice plant cannot tolerate frost, which makes it difficult to grow successfully in cold climates.
- It is not possible to convert an existing wetland into a productive rice paddy.
- Rice is a heavy-feeding grain and requires adequate nitrogen, phosphorous, and potassium.
- Collateral nutrient-rich storm water from animal paddocks (coral or enclosure) can enhance the operation of a rice paddy.

- 90% of rice is produced in Asia. Given the large population of Asia, it is understandable why rice is viewed erroneously as Chinese food.
- To actualize its long-shelf life, cultivated rice should be stored at 14-15% moisture.
- Demonstrating its worldwide appeal, hundreds of Youtube videos are available on the Internet on how to cook rice. Online guides are useful for amateur rice cooks, who just never get the amount of water right. It always seems like there is not enough water; but then the novice cook overcompensates and the rice drowned in water and turns out mushy.
- Cooking rice looks deceptively simple, but it actually thrives in complexity to achieve various cooked outcomes.
- Until the advent of modern technology, the large-scale cultivation of rice required areas with low labor costs and high levels of rainfall.
- Rice production is traditionally labor intensive and requires large amounts of rice for cultivation.
- Rice grains can serve as excellent drying agents for wet items, such as a cell phone that is inadvertently dropped in water.
- Rice is an annual plant that is harvested once a year.
- Small rice seedlings are hand planted into rice paddies that are then filled with water.
- As food is needed to sustain life, we, by induction, need rice somewhere in the spectrum of our culinary habits.
- There are over 40,000 different types of rice. You only need to visit an Asian grocery story to behold the colorful tapestry of bags of rice.
- In terms of nutritional contents, rice is a complex carbohydrate without sodium or cholesterol and barely any fat.
- A fascinating science of rice is that it weighs three times its original weight after it is cooked.
- Rice is a hydrophilic (water-loving) crop.
- Around 96% of rice eaten was produced in that same area of consumption. This is counterintuitive, considering the healthy global import-export trades of rice.

- To affirm the title of my rice poem in the opening chapter (Rice of My Soul), rice has been sustaining human souls for millennia.
- One myth is that Rice Paper is made from rice. Rice paper is actually an umbrella term used to collectively refer to several paper-like materials from East-Asia made from various plants. Vietnamese rice paper is one good example that is made from various indigenous plants.
- As a non-myth fact, rice wine is the Eastern alcoholic beverage made from rice. It originated from China.
- Rice wine is made from the fermentation of rice starch that has been converted to sugars.
- Rice vinegar is used in a lot of Asian cooking because of its mild acidity and hint of sweetness compared to conventional Western vinegar.
- Brown rice is the most nutritional of the various forms of rice.
- Brown rice retains the bran (nutrients) because it is not milled like white rice, which loses a lot of nutrients in the milling process.
- White rice is often enriched to replace the nutrients lost in the milling process. Thus, both brown and white rice are considered good for good health.
- Rice is the second highest worldwide production after corn (maize). However, since maize is often grown for non-human-consumption purposes, rice takes the top spot as the most important grain for human consumption.
- Medium-grain or short-grain rice varieties are more suited to temperate climates.
- Long-grain rice grow well in the tropics.
- Rice seeds are difficult to procure. Many countries have strict restrictions on the importation of rice seeds for agricultural protection reasons.
- Rice seeds germinate best at about 80-90 degrees Fahrenheit.
- In Thailand folklore, family members are called to a meal with the plea of "eat rice." What a sweet sonnet for rice lovers!

- In some Chinese traditions, a young girl is told to eat all the rice on her plate; otherwise each uneaten grain of rice will represent each pockmark on the face of her future husband.

Common Types of Rice

Basmati: Long-grain rice with a unique flavor; common in Indian cuisine.

Jasmine: Long-grain variety of rice that has an aroma of perfume, producing a natural fragrance to a meal.

Long-grain white rice: Refined white rice with a neutral flavor.

Abrorio: Short-grain white rice, which produces sticky rice when cooked.

Whole grain brown: Rice with the bran part retained.

Black sticky: Rice that cooks up sticky and with a dark sheen.

Parboiled rice: Parboiled rice (also called converted rice) is rice that has been partially boiled (par-boiled) in the husk. The three basic steps of parboiling are soaking, steaming and drying. Parboiled rice has more fiber than regular white rice and it is cooked and served just like regular rice. Due to its special processing, parboiled rice is a better source of fiber, calcium, potassium and vitamin B-6 than regular white rice.

Chapter 4

Other Uses of Rice

Rice is not only a smart choice for your palate, but also a great choice for other uses as well. As a versatile crop, rice finds other uses around the home. Rice purists, like I am, find creative ways to use rice in addition to the conventional culinary practices. However, I do not advocate all the uses listed here. My preference is to eat all grains of rice that come my way.

Rice loves water. This fact has led to other uses of rice. For example, if your cell phone gets wet, the easy and fast way to dry it is to cover it in a "bath" of dry rice. The rice will soak up the water from the nooks and crannies of the cell phone. Thus, rice isn't just for culinary consumption. It can also keep your feet warm. It can be called to service as a cleaning agent. Some favorite examples collected over the years are provided in this chapter.

Use rice to clean objects
Use can use rice to clean vases and bottles with slender and unusually shaped profile. Drop in a couple tablespoons of rice, pour in some warm water, and let it soak for about 10 minutes. Then shake vigorously. Then pour it out and rinse the object.

Use rice to clean wet electronics
If your cell phone or another small electronic object accidentally gets dropped in water, remove the battery, if possible, and bury the item in

a bed of rice grains. The rice does its scientific magic by soaking out the wetness the same way it soaks up water during cooking.

Use rice to make a juggling ball

As an alternative to a bean bag, you can fill a small satchel with rice and sew it up niftily to make a juggling ball.

Use rice to clean coffee and spice grinders

Cover the offending area with rice and run it through the grinder. The rice will voraciously absorb a lot of the buildup. This works especially well with instant rice!

Use rice to check if oil is hot enough

If you want to check the temperature of the oil you plan to use for deep frying, drop a grain of rice into it. If the rice pops up to the surface of the oil and begins cooking, the oil is ready for frying. This is a marvel.

Use rice to bake a perfect pie

Instead of using commercial pie weights, the little beads placed on unfilled pie crusts when you blind bake them, use rice filling as a substitute.

Use rice to keep salt flowing freely

A classic restaurant trick is to put a few grains of rice in the salt shaker to prevent the salt from clumping.

Use rice to ripen fruit faster

Store a fruit in a container of rice to expedite the ripening process. Check on the fruit frequently to avoid over-ripening. You can still cook and eat the rice afterwards. In this method, rice concentrates the fruit's ethylene gas, a natural plant hormone that causes fruits to turn softer and sweeter. It is similar to putting a fruit in a paper bag to accelerate ripening.

Use rice to make rice milk

Make rice milk using only the ingredients of rice, salt, and water.

Use rice to make a heating pad

To make a do-it-yourself heating pad, sew a little pouch with a natural fabric like cotton or wool. Fill the pouch up with some rice and sew it shut. You can also use an old sock instead of a self-sewn pouch. Put the home-made heating pad in a microwave. It should stay warm for up to an hour.

Use rice to give your skin a healthy lift

Use leftover cooked rice to rejuvenate your skin. Refrigerate to save it. When needed, warm it and use to it wash your skin. Apply it with a washcloth and rinse. For this skin treatment, brown rice is even better than white rice. Brown rice is high in vitamin E and will give your skin that healthy treatment. Personally, I don't favor this type of wasteful use of rice. All leftover rice should be eaten.

Use rice to sharpen blender blades

Fill a blender with a half cup of uncooked white rice and pulse for about two minutes.

Use rice to prevent tools from getting rusty

Placing some uncooked white rice in an open container in a toolbox will absorb moisture and prevent the tools from rusting.

Use rice to clean thin-necked bottle

Fill the bottle about half to three quarters full with warm (not hot) water and put in 1-2 tablespoons of uncooked white rice. Cover the bottle opening with a cork, cap, stopper, or your finger and shake. Repeat until the bottle is clean.

Use rice to clean coffee grinder or spice grinder

Coffee beans give off oil that is hard to get out of the grinder. Fill the grinder to a level just over the blade with uncooked white rice and run until the rice has been processed through.

Use rice to make hot or cold pack

Fill a pouch (e.g., a small pillow case) with long grain dry rice and sew or tie the opening shut. Put the pack in the microwave to heat for a few minutes and use it as a hot pack. For a cold pack, place the pack in the freezer for a few hours. For a hot pack, exercise caution by heating the pack in about 30-second increments to reach the desired temperature.

Making Glue from Rice Starch

- 3/4 cup of water
- white vinegar
- rice starch
- syrup
- 3/4 cold water

1. mix the 3/4 cup of water with the syrup and the white vinegar and then stir for 10 seconds. Then boil for 1 minute.
2. Mix the rice starch with cold water in a different pan. Again stir for 10 seconds.
3. Slowly add the rice starch with white vinegar and the syrup. And then stir the mixture for 10 seconds. Then boil the mixture for 1 minute. Stir continuously while boiling until the mixture has a thick consistency. Let the mixture cool down and then place in a closed container for one day.

Chapter 5

Rice Kitchen Physics

What is physics? True to the title of this book, "Kitchen Dynamics: The Rice Way," this chapter presents a brief account of physics in the context of what happens in the kitchen.

Physics is the branch of science that tells us what we can and cannot do. It is the science of our actions. In the context of this book, that is kitchen actions. In other words, physics is the science of our actions. As long as we perform actions in the kitchen, physics is, indeed, applicable in our kitchen. The quote below aptly describes the connectivity.

> "What yeast has wrought, let heat manifest. Heat and steam provide the beat; all the meat has to do is dance in the pot." - Deji Badiru (From "Physics in the Nigerian Kitchen," 2010)

> "Biology determines what we are, Chemistry explains what makes us what we are, and Physics describes what we do." - Deji Badiru (From "The Physics of Soccer," 2010)

My website, www.physicsofsoccer.com, presents a basic framework for applying physics in many of our day-to-day activities. For example, Newton's Laws of Motion are echoed below.

Newton's First Law of Motion:

An object at rest tends to stay at rest and an object in motion tends to stay in motion with the same speed and in the same direction unless acted upon by an unbalanced force.

The first law is, perhaps, the most readily observable in the kitchen and elsewhere. A person already in motion will more easily continue to be in motion and be able to "spring" into action in response to events in the kitchen. A person who is stationary will have a more difficult time responding to mobile events in the kitchen. For general health and fitness purposes, being in frequent motion (rather than sedentary practices) is essential for building a healthy lifestyle, in combination with a healthy diet. If you sit around, your body will accommodate sitting around. If you stay active, your body will embrace and accept active lifestyles. So, under the First Law, you may ask "what makes a tick tick?" The "flow of blood," one might say.

Newton's Second Law of Motion:

The acceleration of an object as produced by a net force is directly proportional to the magnitude of the net force, in the same direction as the net force, and inversely proportional to the mass of the object. This is represented in equation form as Force = Mass times Acceleration. In a kitchen analogy, an action taken in the direction of the intended placement of an item requires effort (force) to be applied by the actor. Jettisoning a soiled kitchen utensil from across the kitchen into the sink is a good example that readers can imagine.

Newton's Third Law of Motion:

Newton's Third Law of Motion states that for every action, there is an equal and opposite reaction. A force is a push or a pull upon an object that results from its interaction with another object. Forces result from interactions between objects. According to Newton, whenever objects A and B interact with each other, they exert forces upon each other. When a cook sits in a kitchen chair, his or her body exerts a downward force on the chair, and the chair exerts an upward force on his or her body. There are two forces resulting from this interaction: a force on the chair and a force on the body. These two forces are called *action* and *reaction* forces in Newton's third law of motion. One key thing to remember is that inanimate objects, such as walls, can push and pull back on an object, such as a soccer ball. For a manifestation of this law, think of actions and reactions in a kitchen.

The Thermodynamics of Food Preparation

Cooking is all about the science of physics and chemistry. Over the centuries, humans have learned how to exploit the natural phenomenon of energy transfer through heat for the purpose of transforming food from one form (usually raw) to another form (usually cooked) to facilitate the experience of food consumption.

Thermodynamics is the science of heat transfer between two objects. Heat and steam provide the beat, to which molecules of ingredients dance to create gastronomical delights for dining tables around the world. Like the opening quote above indicates, Biology, Chemistry, and Physics play direct and intertwining roles in our existence and activities, including gastronomic pursuits. To galvanize ingredients to create a marvel for the palate is, indeed, a testimony to the inner workings of science, fueled by fire, steam, and molecules. The transformation from solid to liquid to vapor makes physics in the kitchen fun and gratifying.

Food is primarily composed of water, fat, protein, carbohydrates, and, unfortunately, impurities too. Cooking is the process of transferring energy, usually heat, from an energy source to the food long enough to change its chemistry to achieve a desired level of flavor, texture, tenderness, juiciness, appearance, and nutrition while ensuring safety and digestibility.

Modes of Heat Transfer

Food preparation, whichever way we slice it, requires heat transfer from one source to the other. The heat-source-and-sink relationship has been the keystone of food preparation for centuries. Modern processes have advanced and simplified the heat-source-to-food interface. It is through an appropriate use of heat that food undergoes metamorphosis from one form to another. Intermediate stages of this metamorphosis can exhibit their own rights in terms of food texture, aroma, flavor, and taste. There are five primary modes of heat transfer:

1. Induction
2. Radiation
3. Convection
4. Conduction
5. Excitation

Whether indoor cooking or outdoor cooking, heat transfer is still the primary physics of getting our foods ready for consumption. In communal ethnic village kitchens around the world, the locals have understood the practical principles of utilizing heat transfer in its various forms for a long time, well before written guidance came along.

Induction heating is the process of heating an electrically conducting object (usually a metal) by electromagnetic induction, where currents are generated within the metal and resistance leads to heating of the metal. An induction heater consists of an electromagnet, through which a high-frequency alternating current (AC) is passed. Heat may also be generated by magnetic *hysteresis*, a phenomenon in which magnetic materials show a resistance to any fast-paced changes in their magnetic level. This resistance creates friction, which contributes to the cooking heat. The frequency of AC used depends on the object size, material type, coupling (between the work coil and the object to be heated) and the penetration depth. Some modern rice cookers take advantage of the science and technology of induction heating. While other rice cookers apply heat directly from an electrical plate underneath the inner cooking pan, induction-heating rice cookers get their heat from an alternating electric current from the electric power source. Induction heating, used for many applications beyond rice cookers, is achieved when this current passes through metal coils, typically made of copper. The movement of the current through these coils creates a magnetic field. It is into this magnetic field that the rice cooker's pan is inserted. The magnetic field produces an electrical current inside the cooking pan, and this generates heat. Induction heating improves rice cookers in three main ways:

- The temperature-sensing methods can be more accurate, allowing for fine-tuned adjustments in temperature.
- The heat distribution area can encompass the inner cooking pan, not just radiate upwards from below, to produce more evenly cooked food.
- The level of heat being created in the cooking pan can be changed in an instant by strengthening or weakening the magnetic field that is generating it.

Induction is the latest technology used in stove tops. A copper coil is placed under a smooth cooktop and an alternating current is sent through the coil creating a rapidly changing electromagnetic field. Electrons in conductive steel or cast iron pots placed above the electromagnet are jostled by the rapidly changing magnetism. The electrons exhibit resistance, which gets them to become hot. The pot then conducts the heat to the food without the cooktop or the air around it getting hot. Induction is very responsive to the control knob of the stove and it is extremely energy efficient, but it does not work well with aluminum, glass, or copper pots. This is often baffling to homeowners who complain that certain pots don't cook as fast as others in their kitchen. Lesson to remember: Aluminum, glass, and copper don't conduct heat very well for induction cooking purposes.

Radiation heating is the transfer of heat by direct exposure (without actual touching) to a source of energy. Grilling a hamburger directly over hot coals is cooking mostly with radiant heat with the exception of the parts touching the hot grates. Radiation heating is the reason that nuclear bombs are so destructive.

Convection heating is when heat is carried to the food by a fluid such as air, water, or oil. Cooking a sausage on kitchen oven, where it is surrounded by hot oil, is convection heating. Hot oil, as a medium of convection heat transfer is more effective than using hot air because oil is denser than air and it packs more heat per inch than air. Deep frying a turkey is convection heating. However, the interior of the turkey is cooked by conduction as the heat travels through it without it directly touching the hot oil.

Conduction heating occurs when heat is transferred to the food by contact with the heat source. For example, cooking a sausage in a frying pan is conduction heating. Conduction happens as the surface of the meat gets hotter than the interior and the heat transfers to the center through the moisture and fats. As with most natural processes, heat flows from a region of high concentration to a region of lower concentration. The grill marks on food are caused by conduction heating due to actual touching of the food with the heated surface.

Excitation heating is how microwave ovens work. Microwaves are radio waves that penetrate the food and vibrate the molecules *inside* the food until it gets hot without heating the air around it. Water heats first in the microwave. Technically, this can also be viewed as a form of radiant heat cooking because the molecules get excited, agitated, and highly mobile due to the radiant impact of radio waves.

Traditional cooking in Africa takes advantage of all the different forms of heat transfer described above, albeit in their local and unrefined forms. While the indigenous cooking approaches might not have been recognized in their scientific names, as enumerated above, they are, nonetheless, inherently scientific in their impacts and outputs. The physics of cooking is the same all over the world. The Appalachian (USA) outdoor cooking scenes in the frontier days are very much like the village cooking scenes in Africa.

Common Cooking Methods

If you cook by the wrong method, a tender cut of meat can turn out tough and undesirable.

If you cook by the right method, a tough cut of meat can turn out tender. It is in the science!

We have a multitude of options for cooking our foods. We cannot complain . . . or we should not. Below are the common methods of cooking. Permutations and combinations of the methods are often used to achieve specific cooking objectives. Each method, or combinations thereof, has its own unique physics and chemistry impacts on the food. The interplay of temperature and pressure plays a significant role in cooking.

Baking: This is cooking with dry heat in an enclosed contraption such as an oven or in a large covered pot.

Barbecue (Barbeque, BBQ, Bar-B-Q, Bar-B-Que, Bar-B-Cue, 'Cue, 'Que, Barbie): Barbecue is the oldest cooking method and has been practiced in Africa, Europe, and Asia since the beginning of humans. It involves throwing meat onto hot coals or hanging it above the hot coals. The options for fueling the barbecue heat include wood, charcoal, wood pellets, and gas.

Blanching: In this, foods are submerged in boiling water for a very short time, usually less than five minutes, and then they are usually moved to cold water. The process is used to partially cook a food, to loosen skins on nuts to make them easy to remove, or to make green vegetables become bright green.

Boiling: This is cooking by submerging in boiling water. The bubbles in the boiling water are steam rising to the surface of the hot water. Water boils at 212°F (100°C) at sea level and once it hits that temp it does not rise any higher, no matter how much heat is applied. Boiling temperatures decrease as you go up in altitude because the column of air on top of the liquid is shorter and exerting less pressure so it is easier for water vapor, in the form of steam, to escape. In a high-altitude location, water will boil at some lower temperature. For example, in Denver, the boiling temp of water is about 203°F. We cannot make liquids boil faster by increasing the heat. Boiling is a very severe method of cooking and can easily damage food by breaking down its structure and squeezing out its moisture. Thus, boiled meat can become dry, particularly if aired out after the boiling process.

Braising: This is a wet method of cooking similar to stewing, poaching, or simmering, but the food is usually not submerged as they are in those methods. It is only partially covered in hot, but not boiling liquid for a long time, perhaps 6 to 12 hours. Braising is usually done in large pots, such as Dutch ovens and slow cookers, with the lid not on tight. This keeps the food in the air cooler than the 212°F of the liquid, and allows it to tenderize without drying out as easily.

Broasting®: This is a trademarked method of cooking chicken and other foods using a pressure fryer and condiments. The technique was invented and marketed by the **Broaster Company** of Beloit, Wisconsin. Broasting equipment and ingredients are marketed only to food service and institutional customers, including supermarkets and fast food restaurants. They are not available to the general public. The method essentially combines pressure cooking with deep frying chicken that has been marinated and breaded. The resulting chicken is said to be crisp on the outside and moist on the inside, i.e., like traditional fried chicken but less greasy. Another advantage of broasting over deep-frying is that large quantities of chicken can be prepared more quickly, 12–13 minutes instead of 20.

Broiling: This is direct heat cooking with flame. It is similar to grilling. In recent years the meaning has been confused, and many people refer to broiling as when the flame is directly above the food, but technically it can be either above or below.

Char broiling: This is broiling over charcoal. The grill manufacturer, Char-Broil, makes more gas grills than charcoal grills.

Curing: This is like cooking, but not quite. Although heat is not necessary to cure meats (actually usually done at cool temps), curing is like cooking in that it changes the chemistry of the meat. Curing involves the preservation of meat by the heavy application of some or all of the following: Salts, sugars, nitrates, nitrites, or smoke. Each works differently by altering meat chemistry, inhibiting some microbial growth while promoting others, altering enzymatic digestion, changing the color, and of course, flavoring the meat.

Deep frying: This is cooking at a high temperature, usually 350 to 360°F, by submerging in oil or fat. This method creates more heat than boiling. The high heat creates steam within the food which cooks it and creates pressure at the interface between the food and oil preventing the oil from penetrating if the temperature is properly set. Deep fried foods are usually crisp on the exterior and moist in the interior. Because deep fried foods are often dipped in starch or batter, they can be extra crispy. However, the batter can absorb significant oil, which may not be healthy eating.

Drying: This is the process of dehydrating food by warming it slightly in a low humidity, high airflow environment. It is an excellent method of food preservation since most microbes need water to thrive.

Freeze drying: This is done by freezing the food in a low pressure environment, and then a small amount of heat is applied to sublimate (evacuate, evaporate, remove) the moisture.

Grilling: This is cooking with direct heat over flame or directly over a heat source. Grilling is usually hot and fast cooking.

Microwave Cooking: This is a fast and convenient method of cooking, whereby excitation of molecules in the food is accomplished through microwaves. Molecules deep inside the food vibrate and heat up without heating the air around it. The effect is similar to steaming. There is no dry heat to create the Maillard effect, which is the flavorful crusting of the meat surface. As the surface of foods heat above 310°F, a reaction of amino acids and sugars occur, forming a multitude of new compounds (i.e., organic chemistry), and the surfaces start to brown. This is the Maillard reaction. It creates a richness and depth of flavor and a crunchy texture. It is through the Maillard effect that steaks get grill marks, roasts develop a bark, bread loaves form crusts, slices of bread turn golden in the toaster, coffee beans turn dark when roasted, and fried potatoes darken. The sugar compounds formed also begin to caramelize, producing an appealing appearance of the food.

Pan Roasting: In this method of cooking, the cook starts with a piece of meat, often a thick piece of fish, by browning and crisping the exterior in a thin layer of hot oil in a frying pan. But the meat is still uncooked in the center. The cook then puts the pan in the oven to finish cooking. The result is food that is fried on the top and bottom and baked in the center.

Planking: This is a combination method of indirect cooking, especially popular with salmon. A wood plank, usually untreated western red cedar, which is porous and aromatic, is soaked in water. The food is placed on top of the plank and the plank is placed over direct heat in a closed oven. The plank heats the food by conduction, the water creates steam, the underside of the plank burns creating smoke, and the food roasts in the closed environment. Thus, we have a combination of conduction, steaming, smoking and roasting. Note that construction woods should never be used for planking because they can be treated with toxic chemicals as preservatives.

Poaching: This is similar to stewing, but poaching is usually done in water, or water with just a little salt and/or vinegar added.

Pressure Cooking: Pressure cookers are heavy sealed pots with a locking lid and a high pressure release valve. A small amount of moisture is placed with the food in the cooker. As the pot heats up, moisture and pressure build up. The boiling point of water rises as pressure builds. So, the food cooks at a higher temp and, thus, faster than when steaming under normal pressure. The resulting food resembles braised or simmered food.

Roasting: Traditionally, this is a method of cooking in the open in front of an open flame. Nowadays, it is often done in an enclosed oven with medium to high heat, such as in baking. Customarily, the food is exposed to heat only on one side at a time. But, nowadays, the food is usually surrounded by dry heat and it browns with the Maillard effect and caramelizes evenly. Food can be roasted on a grate, in a pan, on a skewer, or other food holders.

Rotisserie: This is a form or roasting where the food rotates in front of or above a flame so that the meat gets hot on one side and then cools and gets hot again, in an iterative process. Some of the heat is absorbed into the food and some dissipates in the air. The interior cooks evenly.

Sautéing: This is a method of cooking food in a small amount of fat or oil over a high heat on a hot metal surface, usually in a frying pan or skillet, with the goal of rapid cooking and browning. This method helps the food retain moisture and helps prevent it from absorbing oil. To be successful it is important the food is not too cold, the surface of the food must be dry, and the pan cannot be crowded. Sautéing onions and garlic reduces their bite and pungency, and converts some of the compounds to sugar giving them a form of sweetness.

Simmering: This is a slow cooking process under low heat. It is usually done after a period of high-heat cooking.

Smoking: This is a way to cook, flavor, or preserve food by exposing it to smoke, usually from wood, corncobs, tea, and herbs. In the days before refrigeration, smoking was a widely used method of food preservation. But it is not good for all foods since smoke does not penetrate very far into the food. **Cold smoking** is usually done at temperatures under 125°F. The food is heavily infused with smoke flavor, but it is not cooked by heat. This method requires specialize expertise to do it right. Unless done properly, microbes can thrive in the low-temperature of cold smoking, thus increasing the risk of food that is dangerous. For this reason cold smoked meats are often heavily salted, brined, or otherwise cured. Cold smoking of meats should not be done at home. It should be done professionally. Most commercial smoked fishes and cheeses are cold smoked. **Hot smoking** is usually done at temperatures in the 165 to 200°F range. These foods are often also brined or cured. Most American smoked hams are hot smoked. **Smoke roasting** is usually done in the vicinity of 200 to 250°F. The food is cooked by the heat, and when it is finished it is free of harmful living microbes. At these temperatures not much shrinkage occurs. Smoke roasting is relatively easy to do on backyard smokers and barbecue equipment. Most of the best barbecued ribs, pulled pork, and briskets are done with smoke roasting.

Sous-vide: This is French for "under vacuum" and it means putting the meat in a vacuum sealed plastic bag and immersing it in water at the desired serving temperature for hours, even days! It is similar to poaching but more flexible. The process also prevents liquids from escaping, and some chefs add butter or sauce to the bag to build more flavor. Meats come out uniform in color and texture throughout, so they are sometimes seared after cooking to create a Maillard effect crust. Sous-vide must be done correctly because it possesses a deadly risk of developing botulism.

Steaming: In steaming, the food is placed in an enclosed container above boiling water. Steam penetrates the food. It is a very effective method of tenderizing and moisturizing and it is fast. Crabs are often the beneficiaries of this type of cooking.

Stewing: In this method of preparation, food is cooked under a water-based liquid at medium temperatures, usually between 160 to 211°F. Stewing usually is a slow cooking process. Stewed meats are usually browned by sautéing or broiling first to add flavor. These methods can be done in a pot over a heat source or in a slow cooker. The liquids are usually flavored with stock, wine, vegetables, herbs, etc. Ethnic African and Asian stews are famous for their variety, taste, and invigorating aromas.

Stir frying: This is similar to sautéing, but the food is cooked in a curved pan called a wok, and the food is often not browned. Stir frying is often done with a toss of various ingredients, all dancing to the tune of aromatic interactions and enmeshing while the pan stirs.

Surface frying: This method of cooking is frying in a thin layer of oil on a hot metal surface, much like sautéing, but usually on a griddle. Only one surface at a time fries as opposed to deep frying. Specialty burgers are usually prepared this way.

Sweating: Sweating is like sautéing, but done at much lower temperatures. Food is placed in a pot or pan with enough fat or oil to coat it but cooked at low temperatures until it softens or wilts. In other words, the food sweats out its internal moisture.

Infrared Cooking

Infrared (IR) light is electromagnetic radiation with longer wavelengths than those of visible light. The infrared range of wavelengths corresponds to a frequency range that includes most of the thermal radiation emitted by objects near room temperature. Infrared light is emitted or absorbed by molecules when they change their rotational-vibrational movements. Much of the energy from the Sun arrives on Earth in the form of infrared radiation. Out of the energy of the sun reaching the Earth, portions are in infrared radiation, visible light, and ultraviolet radiation. Infrared light is used in industrial, scientific, medical, and more recently, cooking applications. Night-vision devices using infrared illumination allow people or animals to be observed without the observer being detected. In astronomy, imaging at infrared wavelengths allows observation of objects obscured by interstellar dust. Infrared imaging cameras are used to detect heat loss in insulated systems, observe changing blood flow in the skin, and overheating of electrical apparatus.

Infrared is energy radiation with a frequency below the sensitivity of our eyes. So, we cannot see an infrared wave, but we can very well feel it as heat on our skin. With so much energy, infrared is well suited for cooking purposes albeit with a proper design and control of the cooking apparatus. Infrared rays penetrate the food to provide the cooking effect.

Senses for Food Appreciation

Humans are endowed with complex and sophisticated biological sensors to provide a constant stream of environmental information, including position, orientation, and taste among many others. Food can be appreciated and enjoyed via any of the five senses of the human physiological makeup.

Touching: Experience the textual excellence of food.

Hearing: Hear the sizzle of cooking food and sensually get your palates ready.

Smelling: Feel the inviting aroma of food and imagine what is about to transpire.

Seeing: The sight of the visual presentation of food can make the food appetizing and make a person to salivate in anticipation.

Tasting: It is through tasting that the gratification of food is manifested.

Through the sense of taste, humans have four primary discernments of food, namely bitter, sweet, sour, and salty. Our likes and dislikes are shaped by our inherent reactions to our savory perception of food.

For example, the love of chocolate is one avenue through which many people exercise all the senses of appreciation. Consider the comedic quotes below:

> "A new British survey has revealed that 9 out of 10 people like chocolate. The tenth lies." - Robert Paul

"After about 20 years of marriage, I'm finally starting to
scratch the surface of what women want. And I think
the answer lies somewhere between conversation and
chocolate." - Mel Gibson

It is fortuitous that we do have the discerning tastes because many of
the things we savor are good for our health. Unfortunately, some are
counter-productive to health. Tasty fat is one such adverse example.
Salt, for another example, adds palate satisfaction to food while
also meeting a basic requirement of adding an essential nutrient
to our diet. Without the mineral provided by salt, humans cannot
survive. Studies have shown that extreme low-sodium diets pose
risks of possibly suffering from seizures and coma. Other studies have
theorized that the love of the taste of chocolates has the side benefit
of increasing metabolism, thus playing a role in weight loss. A 2012
study found that people who ate chocolates tend to weigh less. It is
suspected that nutrients in chocolate may play a role in metabolism.

French Appreciation of Foie Gras

Many people consider Foie Gras tabu. **Foie gras,** which is French for
"fat liver" is a food product made of the liver of a duck or goose that has
been specially fattened through corn force-feeding, which is known
as gavage. Foie gras is a popular and well-known delicacy in French
cuisine. Its flavor is described as rich, buttery, and delicate, unlike
that of an ordinary duck or goose liver. Foie gras is sold whole, or is
prepared into mousse, parfait, or pastry and may also be served as an
accompaniment to another food item, such as steak. French law states
that "Foie gras belongs to the protected cultural and gastronomical
heritage of France." The technique of gavage is said to date as far
back as 2500 BC, when the ancient Egyptians began keeping birds
for food and deliberately fattened the birds through force-feeding.
Today, France is by far the largest producer and consumer of foie gras,
though it is produced and consumed worldwide, particularly in other

European nations, the United States, and China. Gavage-based foie gras production is controversial due to the force feeding procedure used. A number of countries and other jurisdictions have laws against force feeding or the sale of foie gras.

The French appreciation of foie gras is a testimony that foods that border on being gross and unpleasant in one culture may, indeed, be coveted delicacies in another culture. Examples of such foods abound in most African and Asian cuisine. These include goat intestines, sheep brains, beef tongue, bull testicles, snake gallbladder, fermented cod fish (stockfish), and so on.

Molecular Gastronomy

Molecular gastronomy is a scientific discipline that studies the physical and chemical processes that occur while cooking. Molecular gastronomy seeks to investigate and explain the chemical reasons behind the transformation of ingredients, as well as the social, artistic and technical components of culinary and gastronomic phenomena in general. For example, molecular gastronomy includes the study of how different cooking temperatures affect eggs.

There are many branches of food science, all of which study different aspects of food such as safety, microbiology, preservation, chemistry, engineering, physics and the like. Until the advent of molecular gastronomy, there was no formal scientific discipline dedicated to studying the processes in regular cooking as done in the home or in a restaurant. The aforementioned have mostly been concerned with industrial food production and while the disciplines may overlap with each other to varying degrees, they are considered separate areas of investigation.

Though many disparate examples of the scientific investigation of cooking exist throughout history, the creation of the discipline of molecular gastronomy was intended to bring together what had previously been fragmented and isolated investigation into the chemical and physical processes of cooking into an organized discipline within food science to address what the other disciplines within food science either do not cover, or cover in a manner intended for scientists rather than cooks.

Culinary Physics

Much of the culinary invention in recent decades has been a result of trial and error rather than rigorous scientific research. Serendipity is a common occurrence in cooking. Culinary physics explains the structure and characteristics of food. An example is the classic emulsion process, whereby a liquid is dispersed into another liquid. With a greater understanding of the physical parameters of food, we will know more about how to manipulate them to the extent of our gastronomic desires.

Measurement of Spiciness

Many ethnic cuisines are inherently spicy. But how do we measure how spicy a food is? There is a science for that! Almost all segments of the country indulge in spicy foods as it is believed that a tongue that can withstand the spice demonstrates the owner's path to a clear soul. Depending on the tasters resilience, hot spices can blur the line between pleasure and pain. So, how hot is spicy hot? The **Scoville scale** is a measurement of the spicy heat (a.k.a piquancy) of a pepper. The number of **Scoville heat units** indicates the amount of capsaicin present. Capsaicin is a chemical compound that stimulates chemoreceptor nerve endings in the skin, especially the mucous membranes. The scale is named after its creator, American chemist Wilbur Scoville, who developed a test for rating the pungency of chili peppers. His method, which he devised in 1912, is known as the

Scoville Organoleptic Test. An alternative method for quantitative analysis uses high-performance liquid chromatography, making it possible to directly measure capsaicinoid content. Capsaicin is the main capsaicinoid in peppers.

Does water always Freeze at 32 degrees?

No. Although the freezing point of water is 32 degrees, there are cases where water does not freeze at that temperature. Sure, ordinary water freezes at 32 degrees. But one case of exception is "supercooling," in which case distilled or purified water may not freeze even below 32 degrees if it is placed undisturbed in the freezer. This is because the process of crystallizing, which is needed for freezing to occur, may not happen in pure water. Impurities, however tiny, and disturbance ripples are needed to initiate crystallization. If the supercooled water is moved, even out of the refrigerator, it immediately begins to freeze. How about that for the wonders of physics!

Can an Apple a day really keep the doctor away?

No, not really. But, yes, to some extent. Read on. An apple a day keeping the doctor away is believed to have come from an ancient Roman proverb. The apple was believed to have magical powers to cure all kinds of illnesses. This is probably because of the proven properties of the

Fiber: Apples are a good source of dietary fiber. Typical measurements reveal about 4 grams of dietary fiber per five ounce apple. This equates to approximately 15% of the recommended daily intake. Apples contain both soluble and insoluble fiber in the form of cellulose and pectin. Both of these fibers have been documented to be beneficial for cholesterol.

Antioxidants and Vitamin C: Unlike animals, humans are unable to synthesize vitamin C in the body. It is, thus, essential to find a good natural source of vitamin C. Apples provide this source. Vitamin C is well known for preventing scurvy through the use of limes by the British Navy during 1795. It is also well known that vitamin C has many immune system enhancing properties and it is, therefore, important for overall health. Vitamin C is also a superb antioxidant, and it is essential for cell detoxification and enzymatic function. Apples also contain bioflavonoids, which are known for their antioxidant properties. Apples contain a long list of phytonutrients, including quercetin, catechin, phlorizin and chlorogenic acid. It is important to note that many of the nutrients of an apple are contained within the apple's skin. Thus, eating the skin is a good practice.

Antioxidants include vitamins A, C, and E as well as the mineral selenium. They are needed by the body for a variety of functions, including protecting against cancer, heart disease, cataracts, diabetes, and retinal failure, just to name a few. In ordinary language, antioxidants are substances or nutrients in foods, which can prevent or moderate the oxidative damage to the body. When cells in the body use oxygen, they naturally produce free radicals or by-products which can cause damage. Antioxidants possess the ability to prevent and repair damage done by free radicals. Common examples of antioxidants, by vitamin categories, are listed below:

Vitamin A: Carrots, squash, broccoli, sweet potatoes, tomatoes, kale, collards, cantaloupe, peaches, apricots, and bright-colored fruits and vegetables.

Vitamin C: Citrus fruits (oranges, lime), green peppers, broccoli, green leafy vegetables, strawberries, and tomatoes.

Vitamin E: Nuts, seeds, whole grains, green leafy vegetables, vegetable oil, and liver oil.

Selenium: Fish, shellfish, red meat, grains, eggs, chicken and garlic.

Other common sources of antioxidants include soy, red wine, purple grapes, concord grapes, cranberries, tea, tomato, pink grapefruit, watermelon, dark green vegetables, spinach, oatmeal, and barley.

Omega-3 Foods

Omega 3 are fatty acids derived from fish (e.g., fish oil), seaweed, flaxseed, and walnuts. Fish Oil is a natural source of Omega-3 fatty acids, which is vital for normal cell growth, and essential fatty acids play a key role in cell health. Omega-3 acids benefit the hearts of healthy people and those at high risk of cardiovascular disease. Salmon, flax seeds, soybeans, halibut, snapper, tofu, and walnuts are excellent food sources of Omega-3 fatty acids.

In a nutshell, Omega-3 fatty acids are healthy fats. For example, polyunsaturated fats, unlike saturated fats, are liquid at room temperature and remain liquid when refrigerated or frozen. Monounsaturated fats, found in olive oil, are liquid at room temperature, but harden when refrigerated. Each type of fat has health benefits depending on how it is prepared, used in recipes, and the amount consumed.

Food Homogeneity

Homogeneous foods exhibit uniform consistency of their properties, including color, texture, taste, and so on. Milk is a good example for explaining homogeneity. Raw milk is usually separated into its various natural components through centrifuge. The components are mixed in various proportions (combinations and permutations) to generate a host of products, such as butter, cream, skim milk, x% milk, and so on. The various milk types are homogenized to prevent their fatty solids from rising to the top of the milk. As every milk product, even skim milk, has some fat content, homogeneity makes it uniform in the final store-shelf properties.

Combinations and Permutations of Rice Dishes

Ingredient variations, combinations, and permutations rule in recipe world. Millions of people experiment with recipes and combinations and permutations of ingredients on a daily basis. Some hit the jackpot of new gastronomic discoveries while many have to go back to the drawing board . . . or shall we say, chopping board. With all these culinary experimentations, it is difficult for anyone to claim a patent on a recipe and expect to retain the rights for long. There are, however, proprietary recipes, such as Coca-Cola˚ and KFC˚ formulas. Other than secret proprietary formulas, recipes are one thing that everybody freely and proudly shares with others. Recipe sharing is the ingredient that can bind the world toward a better cultural understanding.

From basic shared recipes, new combinations and permutations evolve to generate new recipe creations. Consider a test question that requires students to compute the different number of meal choices possible, given a certain set of menu options. This is calculated by the combination and permutation formulas in Statistics. A typical question might ask for how many meal choices are able to a diner if, in a particular restaurant, there are three types of meat, four types of vegetables, five types of drinks, and six types of dessert. In this case, the answer is:

Meal choices = 3(meat options) x 4(vegetable options) x 5(drink options) x 6(dessert options) = 360 unique meal choices

Isn't this amazing? So, when you complain of not having many menu options at a restaurant, you really haven't evaluated the number of combination options available. To extend the computational example further, consider the following. Suppose one and only one particular combination of meat option and drink option will kick in an allergic reaction for a diner, what is the probability that this particular diner can get sick at this particular restaurant if the meal options are selected at random? Using the laws of probability, the answer is calculated as Probability of allergic reaction = 1/360 = 0.002778. That is less than a 0.3 percent chance of this particular diner getting sick at this particular restaurant in a random combination of menu options. Of course, with prior knowledge of the allergic reaction tendencies of the diner, certain menu options can be eliminated from the initial set of options; thereby reducing the probability of getting sick to zero.

The above example can be made even more interesting by extending it to permutation, which is the number of possible arrangements of k objects selected from a pool of n objects. In that case, we may be looking at the order in which the menu options are consumed. For example, we can evaluate eating dessert before eating vegetables versus eating vegetables first. Each order represents a unique permutation. Analyses such as these can open up a whole new world of food for thought when evaluating meal options. Because this book is not about drawing statistical inferences about food options, we will leave further discussions to the imagination of the reader.

Science of Boiling Water

Salt in Water: Boiling water is a cornerstone of cooking rice. So, it helps to understand how water boils, from a scientific point of view. There are several myths and facts about boiling water. Water and salt are two of the most important essentials in a kitchen. It is interesting to note how they interact to do what we expect of them in terms of our food preparation. The effect of salt on the boiling point of water is particularly of interest, but only for theoretical reasons. For practical kitchen applications, the effect is negligible. But for scientific curiosity, we will examine the effect. Adding salt to water increases the boiling temperature (i.e., boiling point), causing the water to come to a boil more slowly. That is, it requires a higher temperature to boil. This increase in the cooking temperature will cause foods boiled in salt water to cook faster. Pure liquids (e.g., water) will generally have lower boiling points than mixtures (e.g., water and salt). For this reason, adding sugar to water has the same increasing effect on the boiling point as adding salt. If pure water is heated up to a high temperature prior to the addition of the salt, it could cause the entire pot to start boiling spontaneously. This is a result of the grains of salt acting as nucleation sites. This has the effect of making nearly-boiling water actually boil more quickly when salt is added. The tiny amount of salt required to cause a nucleation effect would have no effect on the temperature of the boiling water. In this regard, you can think of the salt as a catalyst, facilitating the change of state of the water from liquid to boiling.

Adding salt to water to raise the boiling point for cooking is actually negligible in practice. The amount of salt we normally add to water for typical cooking would have negligible effect on the boiling temperature. To easily remember this relationship, we present the visual plot below, based on a simple lab experiment. For fun experimentation purposes, you can add a few grains of salt to pure water to kick off the boiling process with nucleation; but beyond that, it will not have any noticeable effect on cooking temperature or time.

Salt raises water's boiling point and lowers its freezing point. This means that the water will need to reach a higher temperature before it begins to boil. That is, more salt means more boil time. But, normally, the amount of salt that we usually add to water when cooking is not large enough to make a significant (or even noticeable) difference in the boiling point. From general chemistry, the fact that dissolving a salt in a liquid, such as water, affects its boiling point comes under the general heading of ***colligative*** properties of materials. As a general phenomenon, if you dissolve one substance (the solute, e.g., salt) in another (the solvent, e.g., water), you will raise the boiling point of the solvent. In fact, any non-volatile soluble substance will raise the boiling point of water. That is why antifreeze (ethylene glycol) provides boiling protection in summer as it simultaneously provides freezing protection in the winter.

Sugar in Water: Why does sugar not increase the boiling point of water as much as salt does? The increase in boiling point depends on the number of molecules you add to the liquid. Salt has a very small molecule. In addition it splits into two particles when in water, the sodium atom and the chloride atom. In numbers: if you add 6g of salt into water, you add about 4,400,000,000,000,000,000,000 $(4.4*10^{22})$ particles to the water. Sugar has a molecular weight that is 3 times larger than that of salt. It does not split up in different particles when in water. So adding 6g of sugar into water, you add around 700,000,000,000,000,000,000 particles $(7.3*10^{21})$ to the water. This is still a huge number, but considerably less than with salt. To get the same effect with sugar that you get with salt, you will have to use about 6 times as much sugar as salt. The same is true in principle with lowering the freezing point of liquids. That is the reason why we use salt in winter on our streets and not sugar - as we would need 6 times as much for the same effect. But it would work with sugar too, if you use enough of it.

Hot water freezes faster than cold water: Normally, yes! Under normal circumstances, cold water freezes faster than hot water. However, a strange phenomenon known as the *Mpemba* effect can, under some very specific and obscure conditions, make hot water freeze faster than cold water. One possible explanation is that extremely hot water will lose some of its volume to evaporation, with the result that the smaller quantity of water will freeze faster than a larger quantity. So, technically speaking, this is a fact.

Previously boiled water freezes faster than regular water: Fact. At room temperature, water that was once boiled should freeze faster because the dissolved oxygen has been removed.

Previously boiled water boils faster than regular water: Previously boiled water at room temperature should boil faster than water that has never been boiled. Likewise, previously boiled water freezes faster because of having less dissolved oxygen.

Cold water boils faster than hot water: Myth. Although common sense might suggest that if hot water freezes faster, cold water should boil faster. But that is not the case, scientifically. Hot water from the tap boils faster than cold water, if time saving is the goal. If saving energy is the objective, using hot water for boiling does not actually save much in terms of net energy usage. This is because energy (gas or electricity) is used to heat the water from the tap in the first place, through the hot water heater. On the cautionary side, hot water heaters may even introduce sediments and impurities to the water. For this reason, we are often discouraged from using hot water from the tap for cooking purposes or direct consumption.

Water boils faster at high altitude. Fact. This is due to the effect of lower pressure at high altitude. The higher we go, the lower the pressure. Water expands when it boils. High altitude makes that expansion much more readily possible. This means that large increases in altitude can measurably reduce the boiling temperature. For most substances, the freezing point rises, albeit only very slightly, with increased pressure. Tea connoisseurs often comment that high altitude affects the cooking time of tea as well as its taste. While cooking time can be scientifically verified, the taste assertion must be left to the subjective taste buds of tea aficionados. Water is one of the very rare substances that expand upon freezing. Consequently, the temperature at which ice thaws falls very slightly with increased pressure.

Impact of Humidity on Cooking

Although not often seen as a cooking-related issue, humidity does have an impact on cooking. In addition to temperature and pressure, humidity is perhaps the third-ranking factor in how cooking turns out. Just as temperature determines the burnt or raw outcome of cooked meat, humidity content determines how soggy or dry the outcome is. Cold air contains less moisture (humidity) than warm air. For example, each time you open the freezer, warmer and more humidity-laden air creeps into the freezer due to the process of osmosis. Osmosis is the scientific process through which fluids migrate from a region of higher concentration to a region of lower concentration. In our example, humidity migrates from a higher-humidity ambient room air to the lower-humidity freezer compartment. The newly introduced humid air is cooled off by the freezer, thereby releasing moisture. This cooled air crystallizes and is seen as films of ice on freezer food. When food is stored in a freezer bag, it is protected from this "ice invasion," thus preserving its freshness and freezer life longer. The plastic freezer bag also protects the food from its own natural release (outflow) and intake (inflow) of moisture.

During baking or cooking in a conventional oven, the oven air gets warmed up and rarefied, causing it to be able to absorb more moisture. This dries out the food being cooked. Adding more moisture to the air in the oven can alleviate the drying out problem. We can preheat the oven to the desired cooking temperature and then add a measured amount of water in a crucible to the oven. After the water evaporates through boiling, the food to be cooked can then be placed in the oven. Wrapping food in baking bags helps preserve moisture in the food to minimize unnecessary drying out in the oven. By the way, freezer burn is often the result of excessive drying out of food in the freezer that leaves burn-like scalds on the food.

Impact of Humidity on Personal Comfort

The impact of humidity on personal comfort is much more noticeable and understood than the impact on cooking. For example, let us suppose a central home heating-and-air-conditioning unit operates at 72°F and the temperature is maintained constant through effective thermostat setting. In winter, one may feel too cold while feeling too warm in summer --- both at the same temperature of 72°F. The difference is, of course, due to the impact of relative humidity. When air is dry (less humid), the same temperature feels cooler than it does when the air is moist (more humid). So, in winter, the combination of dry air and 72°F temperature may feel too cold while, in summer, the combination of more humid air 72°F temperature may feel too hot. To remedy this discomfort discrepancy, we use humidifiers in winter and humidifiers in summer.

Kitchen Chemistry

The kitchen is full of chemistry and chemical reactions. In the normal course of things, many of these are rarely recognized as scientific phenomenon by cooks who know intimately how to take advantage of the chemical properties of ingredients. One of the interesting phenomena in the kitchen is the transition of matter from one phase to another, with each phase having a specific role in the kitchen's dance of molecules. Regardless of the type of molecule, matter normally exists as a *solid*, a *liquid*, or a *gas*. Without going scientifically overboard, let us discuss some of the basic aspects of solid-liquid-gas transitions useful for kitchen activities.

Solid-Liquid-Gas Phases

Scientists take delight in studying the different phases of matter, particularly the various temperatures and pressures at which one phase changes into another. Each natural material, even food, for that matter, has three states into which it can transition back and forth. The three states are:

- Solid (e.g., snow, ice)
- Liquid (e.g., rain, lake, stream)
- Gas (e.g., water vapor, fog, cloud, steam)

No kitchen can function without water. But water comes in the three basic forms listed above. The gas state is actually water vapor, which is useful for steaming vegetables and other delicate cooking ingredients. Clouds, snow, and rain are all made of up of some form of water. A cloud is comprised of tiny water droplets and/or ice crystals, a snowflake is an aggregate of many ice crystals, and rain is just liquid water. Water existing as a gas is called water vapor. When referring to the amount of moisture in the air, we are actually referring to the amount of water vapor. If the air is described as "moist," that means the air contains large amounts of water vapor.

Sublimation

In addition to the phase transitions described above, a chemical conversion is also possible through sublimation, which is the process in which a substance is converted directly from a solid to a gas or from a gas to a solid without an intermediate liquid phase.

A solid has a definite shape and volume. A liquid has a definite volume but it takes the shape of a container whereas a gas fills the entire volume of a container. A phase is a distinct and homogeneous state of a system with no visible boundary separating it into parts. Conversion between these states is called a phase transition. Water is the most common substance that its gas (steam), liquid (water), and solid (ice) phases are widely known. An ice water mixture has two phases, so are systems containing ice-and-vapor, and water-and-vapor. To recognize the vapor system in these systems may require a keen observation, because the vapor usually blends with air, and is not detected directly. In a solid the molecules have no motion, and no energy.

The Fourth State of Matter

Plasma is known as the fourth state of matter after the three states of solid, liquid and gas. In most cases, matter on Earth has electrons that orbit around the atom's nucleus. The negatively charged electrons are attracted to the positively charged nucleus. Yes, opposites do attract in the atom world. So, the electrons stay in orbit around the nucleus. When temperatures get extremely hot, the electrons can escape out of their orbit around the atom's nucleus. When the electrons leave the nucleus, they leave behind a positively charged ion. When electrons are no longer trapped in orbits around the nucleus, we have the plasma state. This is when a gas becomes a collection of electrons, which have escaped the pull of the nucleus and ions which are positively charged because they have lost one or more electrons. In the plasma state (aka supercritical state), a substance acts like a gas in some ways and like a liquid in some other ways. Most of the matter in the universe is found in the plasma state. Stars constitute much of the matter in the universe and they are so hot that their matter can only exist in the plasma state. With regard to the above definition of plasma, lightening is best classified as a plasma. We can rest assured that the plasma state does not exist in our kitchens. We certainly hope not.

Food Breadth

Good oral hygiene is an essential part of enjoying your food experiences. Most people associate certain foods with bad breadth. But only in certain cases is this true. Bad breadth is a social embarrassment that happen to anyone because it has diverse causes.

In addition to poor oral hygiene, other possible causes of bad breadth include:

- Bacteria on the tongue
- Dry mouth
- Eating foods with strong odor
- Infection
- Smoking
- Alcohol

As an example, the indigenous Nigerian practice of using herbal chewing sticks to clean teeth has been pharmacologically shown to aid good oral hygiene. Dry mouth is particularly a common, but unrecognized, cause of bad breadth that can happen to anyone. A summary of self-care and preventative practices to wade off bad breadth include the following:

- Prevent dry mouth by keeping the mouth hydrated. Drink plenty of water regularly.
- Eat or chew at regular intervals to keep the mouth moist.
- Practice good oral hygiene by brushing teeth and tongue regularly.
- If applicable, clean dentures and ensure they fit properly in the mouth.
- Don't smoke.
- Limit the consumption of alcohol.
- If possible, use baking soda toothpaste
- Don't rely entirely on mouthwash or mints. They work by masking bad breadth and only provide temporary relief. In some cases, they can actually fuel bad breadth by making the mouth dry.
- Chew sugarless gum.
- Suck on lemon drops, which help make saliva and wash away food particles.
- Eat oranges to moisten and freshen the mouth.

Science of Garlic Breadth

Scientifically, after chewing and swallowing garlic, sulfur-containing gases pass through the gut, then circulate throughout the body. The compounds in garlic are morph into nastier forms. With time, the gases are excreted by the lungs. And they increase acetone in the breath, making it outright pungent. So, when "garlic breath" occurs, it is due to exhaling the smelly gases from the lungs, not from the mouth. No amount of brushing, gargling or chewing red-hot chili peppers can stop the exhaled gases.

Chapter 6

Other Rice Kitchen Dynamics

The kitchen is a special place in all cultures around the world. The best family traditions often start in the kitchen. It is the pathway to our well-being and the channel for a fulfilled soul. As such, it is full of physics and dynamics in the practical sense. In many ethnic kitchens, cooking is often a manifestation of passion rather than a mere necessity. Food is a universal language of well-being. Food sustains life. No one can practice perpetual and complete abstinence from food. Since complete abstinence from food is not possible, we might as well embrace it, celebrate it, and pay homage to all the stages of food transformation; growing it, cultivating it, harvesting it, cooking it, consuming it, digesting it, and using it to nourish our bodies. No matter what your background is, the fact remains that you have a close relationship with food. Cooking is like a well-orchestrated symphony, where carefully appointed ingredients play together in perfect harmony. The symphony director (aka the chef) is the cornerstone of the kitchen.

The modern kitchen has as much drama and sentiments as the communal kitchen common in rural villages of the World. There is a lot of dynamics that occur in every kitchen environment. In a rural communal kitchen, housewives congregate and interact to discuss current affairs in the household and debate community politics, very much like a water cooler gathering point in the Western offices. Each household in the communal compound has its own stove or cooking spot in the shared space. So, the interplay of people, personalities, physical environment, and cooking equipment create memorable kitchen dynamics.

Even in a single-family modern kitchen, where there is no sharing of cooking space, the family structure and residential personalities still create unique kitchen dynamics. But regardless of whichever kitchen structure prevails, the best foods still emanate as the end product. The communal kitchen mentioned earlier is a beehive of activities full of energy and cacophony of laughter, particularly during party preparations. In spite of its chaotic and jumbled appearance, the kitchen puts out the best of the best of food preparation. The term, Physics, in the title of this book, is not just about the science of physics. Rather, the word epitomizes the dynamics (processes, actions, and interfaces) that exist in a kitchen environment. In the rural communal kitchen, commotion is what breeds gastronomic excellence, particularly for large party preparations

Food, Friendship, Family, Fellowship, and Faith

Food is the centerpiece of family, fellowship, and faith in many World cultures. Asians and African take this rallying point to the next level in the way they host and entertain friends, family, neighbors, and extended acquaintances. Cooking and serving food is an essential part of how human promote fellowship. The Ronald Reagan quote below highlights the family fellowship of food in the household.

> "All great change in America begins at the dinner table." – Ronald Reagan

In my own interpretation, this quote is more specifically applicable at the dinner table where rice is served. From the Western, Eastern, Northern, and Southern nooks and corners of the world, food is embraced and even worshiped in some local practices. Just as sports are often used as common basis to unify disparate parts of a developing nation, the common interest in food can also be used as a common basis to overcome the nagging political differences that are rampant in developing nations. Trade and commerce related to food are important elements of how communities and nations interact. From sharing food, exchanging recipes, and *"festivalizing"* food to creating community unions, food facilitates participatory alliances among people of all creed and color throughout the world. Mass feeding of everyone within reach is a trademark of all African chefs, which is a direct demonstration of the passion of cooking for many.

Beyond the Physics

As farmers, even without the benefit of written theory, can tell us, a lot of physics happens in how water moves through a plant's roots, stems, and leaves to generate the unique characteristics that make them edible and delectable. In rice-oriented food cultures, diets consist of many plant products (i.e., roots, stems, and leaves). So, plant physics essentially goes on behind the scene of the kitchen. The topic of physics, whether from the classical theory of physics or the more generic interpretation of dynamics, does play an important role in the kitchen. Therein lies the need to write about physics in kitchen dynamics. Good chefs, even without a formal knowledge of physics, do understand how to leverage the physics in each food source (e.g., water content, permeability, microbial properties, etc.) to achieve their culinary goals. Indigenous cooks, even without any formal education, can cook up a marvel because they understand the inherent properties of their raw materials. That is kitchen physics!

Most ingredients undergo radical scientific transformation before reaching the final flavor at which we use them. In many cases, the intermediate stages of the transformation have their own uses in the cooking process as they can impact different levels of texture, visual appeal, flavor, and taste. For example, it is reported that fresh garlic, when minced can become spicy, however, when slightly sautéed or roasted, it becomes sweet.

The art of cooking relates to the skills of using the various ingredients in tactical combinations to arrive at the intended end goal of a recipe. Finally, it is the passion of cooking that brings out the best in every cook. Without the passion, the cooking effort is a mere abstraction of desire without a manifestation.

Food poisoning is rare in many ethnic cuisines because rarely is anything cooked rare (double pun intended). Most foods are cooked well done. The Western practice of cooking meat rare or medium rare usually doesn't sit well in African cuisine. The practice of multiple hand washings is also common in the African kitchen because bare hands are used constantly throughout the cooking process. From hand-handling of meat to sprinkling of spices on the food, hands must be used again and again. In fact, in the final eating of the food, it is not uncommon to dispense of silverware in favor of digging in with bare fingers. That is actually the best way to enjoy many ethnic delicacies. So, intuitively, hands are washed frequently.

Eating in Moderation

> "Always leave the table feeling like you could have eaten more."
>
> > - Oriental Philosophy

After exercising all the senses of food appreciation, now comes the task of burning off the calories. It is treadmill time! Treadmills are fantastic for indoor calorie burn-off. Accumulated fat that refuses to dissipate of its own accord can be helped along with a good treadmill workout. While it is good to get out and workout in the open air occasionally, indoor treadmill workout offers convenience, privacy, and protection from the weather elements; not to talk of avoidance of neighborhood dogs seeking to "bite out of" joggers.

Food is often the culprit in many of our ailments, either in a wrong form, irrational quantity, or incompatible combination. The fact is that we don't need much food to sustain life. As much as I encourage eating well with diverse experimentations, it is recognized that food must be consumed in moderation. Laboratory studies as well as direct human observations tend to suggest that consistently consuming large quantities of food can adversely affect life span. Not only does a large quantity of food blatantly task the body's digestive system, it also means that whatever unfavorable contents lurk in the food end up bombarding the body mechanisms more aggressively. Over a long stretch of time, these adverse impacts manifest themselves in all sorts of diseases whose root causes are difficult to trace. External impacts can be seen through visual assessment of size (e.g., obesity) while internal impacts are often unnoticeable until it is too late. So, the basic lesson is to experiment with food (cooking, tasting, consuming, etc.), but also give the body a fighting chance against the unwanted side effects that come with some food choices. Eating less not only has positive effect on weight, but also helps to wade off potential sources of pathogens by reducing the type and volume of what is ingested. Below are some quotes that are pertinent to the above discussion.

"Some live to eat, some eat to live." - Source unknown

"...he is a heavy eater of beef. Me thinks it doth harm to his wit." - Shakespeare

"A diet is when you watch what you eat and wish you could eat what you watch." - Hermione Gingold

"A fully gorged belly never produced a sprightly mind." - Jeremy Taylor

"A good meal ought to begin with hunger." - French Proverb

"A hungry stomach seldom scorns plain food." - Horace

The Communal Psychology of Stuffing the Plate

"Things sweet to taste prove is digestion sour." - William Shakespeare

The quote above suggests that not all good things that we eat are good for our body in the long run of running through the stomach (pun intended).

It is obvious that we tend to eat more when we eat with other people and eat less when we eat alone. Of course, we would always have those who eat against the grains in these standardized hypotheses. When you eat less alone, it is probably because you don't have to impress alone with your appetite. When you eat more alone, it is probably because you lack self-discipline and you would gorge yourself if no one is watching. In the case of those who eat more in a group, it is often because of what I would call *competitive cyclic psychology* of filling up the plate. This is how it happens, particularly in smorgasbord restaurants that serve a large variety of buffet items. The first person spies on the second person's plate and thinks 'gee, he got more than I got,' and responds by pilling more food onto his own plate. This sends a subliminal message. Of course, the second person subconsciously notices that he is being beaten in the unspoken and unannounced eating competition and decides to retaliate by piling on more food, possibly from a different variety from the buffet table. This *strike-back* mentality can go on back and forth until each person has overdone it, thereby fueling the wheels of obesity subconsciously. Sometimes it is someone desiring to eat more who gets the competition started. This instigator might say 'is that all you got? Get more, we have plenty of food you know' and it is already paid for. This challenge urges others to fill their plates more. He or she then uses any credulous responders as an excuse to then pile up more food onto his or her own plate.

Children are particularly prone to the type of competitive eating psychology described here. There is a *scarcity mentality* that lurks somewhere in all of us, and it does not apply only to food. It tells us to grab all we can; otherwise, someone else will grab it all. This is very rampant and socially damaging in developing countries where basic resources are in limited supply to begin with. So, how do we combat this psychology of stuffing the plate? My simple advice is to *mind your own plate.* Don't look around the table for benchmarks. And don't be swayed by the clash of gastronomic aroma at the buffet table.

Because of its physical structure of embedded space in-between its grains, rice is particularly an inviting chow to eat more of. Since loose cooked white rice is not compact, the stomach can accommodate more of it. This can lead to an unsuspecting overfilling of the stomach.

One other trick to combat plate-stuffing is to not wait until you are famished before you eat. Eating when you are extremely hungry will lead to eating too much and too fast. Remember, you should always leave the table feeling like you can eat more. This is not just about avoiding weight gain. It is also about not overloading and overlarding your body system. Even though the instant gratification of extreme consumption is pleasing, repeated overloading of the body with food will adversely affect health, quality of life, and longevity.

Body and Taste Bud Conflict: There is often a conflict between what our taste buds want and what our bodies need. To emphasize this, co-author Deji created the original quote below to convey his own perception of this conundrum,

59

> *"Nature has a twisted sense of humor. Whatever is good for our taste buds is often not good for our body."* - Deji Badiru, Dec 30, 2007

It is true that foods that taste the best are not often the best foods for us health-wise. This conjecture is aptly illustrated by popular-press stories of hypothetical taste-and-risk relationships. Diversification is of utmost importance for good life and soul health. Even if you love processed fast foods, just make sure it is not your only staple food source.

General Culinary Experimentations

I advocate more adventurous engagements of cooking rice beyond the conventional recipes and cooking practices. Readers are encouraged to try something new, substitute uncharted ingredients, and experiment with modern healthy choices.

The traditional rice recipes that call for the use of one type of ingredient can be experimented with by using a new ingredient. A bit of this, a dash of that, and a sprinkle of new spices can lead to new recipe discoveries. Husbands should, however, be cautious when conducting recipe experiments in the presence of their wives, unless there a defendable explanation. The following hypothetical conversation between a husband and his wife attests to this suggestion:

Husband:
"Wow, this did not turn out as I hoped."

Wife:
"Wishful thinking does not a good recipe make. You've ruined a perfectly good rice dish."

Husband:
"Well, I learned something new from this cooking experiment."

Wife:
"What lesson could that happen to be?"

Husband:
"Never to try it again; and others can learn from my lesson"

In spite of the failed experiments, don't be shy. Go ahead and try something new. Don't quit too soon. Success could be failure turned inside out. So, try and try again. Culinary success may be lurking in the next pot of rice.

What would have happened if someone so long ago did not experiment to discover the effect of salt on food flavor or the impact of sugar on the taste of tea? How did we discover the kicks of various spices?

Food is a unifying element in family relationships. It brings us together in times of trouble and in times of joy. We celebrate with food. We celebrate food. In a talk about her book, *Recipes for Life,* Dynasty actress Linda Evans says she incorporates memories in her memoir with two of her favorite things --- cooking and eating. It seems to us that she endorses the new movement of "eatertainment."

Of the body, eating provides nourishments that are essential for life, healing, and thriving as a social being. Of the soul, eating offers pleasure that excites the senses that make a person what he or she is spiritually and socially. While the body represents the engagement of time and space, it is the soul that creates the aura that ties everything together. Essentially, the soul is the atmosphere, spiritual or otherwise, within which the body resides. Of the mind, eating expands the mind both through the anticipatory comfort of the food as well as the gratification of going through the action of consumption. A dull mind can result from not being exposed to a wide variety of food.

Temperature and Flavor: Temperature affects flavor. As reported by the November 2012 issue of Reader's Digest, researchers in Belgium found that certain taste bud receptors are most sensitive to food molecules that are at or just above room temperature. So, hot coffee may seem less bitter (i.e., tastes better) because our bitter-detecting taste buds are not as sensitive when coffee is hot. It was also found that odors also influence flavor. Thus, even the most bitter hot coffee may taste delicious because of its pleasant aroma. Coffee at room temperature does not have the same aroma.

Growling Stomach: What makes a stomach growl? It is believed that the digestive chemicals in the stomach churn and make stomach muscles to contract as they get prepped for food. Subconscious mental anticipation can cause muscle reflexes whether you want it or not. Consider the uncontrollable pee-pee urgency that develops as you approach a point of relief (aka the toilet), which can lead to the famous pee-pee dance. To mitigate a growly stomach, eat smaller meals more frequently.

Meat Tips for Rice

- Meats are best if purchased fresh and used the day of, or within a day of purchase
- Always check the "Best if used by" date on the meat packaging for the freshest meats. Meats begin to lose flavor and spoil if you don't use them within 2- 3 days of purchase.
- Look for fat marbling in fresh beef. The fat adds more flavor, juiciness and tenderness to meats. But too much fat is strongly discouraged.
- Meats labeled "Reduced for Quick Sale" should be purchased only if you plan to use the meat the day of purchase. If possible, never buy meats that are out of date. The flavor and safety could be at risk.

- Fresh meat should be stored unwrapped or wrapped loosely in waxed paper, plastic wrap, paper wrap or aluminum foil. This allows the air to partially dry the surface of the meat and retard bacteria growth.
- Cured and smoked meats, sausages and ready-to-serve meats can be stored in their original wrappings.
- Cooked meat should be refrigerated quickly. Do not allow cooked meats to rest at room temperature for extended amounts of time. Room temperature will hasten bacterial growth on cooked meats, as well as uncooked meats.
- Do not freeze canned meats.
- To defrost frozen meats, always allow time to thaw in the refrigerator. Bacteria begins to grow on meats thawing at room temperature, therefore the meat becomes unsafe.
- Frozen meats can be cooked directly from the freezer, but the cooking time should be extended by up to 1/3 the normal amount of time for thawed or fresh meats.
- Using the correct cooking method for meats will optimize flavor and tenderness. This is good physics!
- When slicing meat, always cut **against** the grain of the meat. This will make the slices that are served more tender and easier to chew. Cutting meat with the grain will make meat stringy and it will seem tougher.
- When cutting raw meat, do not re-use the same cutting utensils during the cooking or eating process. Always use separate, clean utensils for raw and cooked meat. When cutting raw meat on a cutting board, do not cut cooked meat on the same board unless it has been washed thoroughly in Hot, Soapy water! Bacteria can be easily transferred to the cooked meat you are about to serve.
- When raw meat is placed on a plate or platter and taken to your outdoor grill, do not place the grilled meat back on the same plate or platter. Either wash the platter in hot, soapy water first, or use a clean platter.
- When marinating meat, discard the leftover marinade after you remove the meat.

- Never serve the raw meat marinade on your cooked meat.
- Some raw meat marinades can be cooked and served after the raw meat has been removed from it. Once a marinade has been cooked, it is safe. The extreme heat during the cooking process will kill any and all possible traces of bacteria that may have grown during the marinating process.

Tips for General Rice Accompaniments

- Fresh eggs have rough, chalky shells. If the shell is smooth and shiny, it's old.
- The whites of poached or boiled eggs won't run if you add a teaspoon of vinegar to the water when boiling.
- To determine if that loose egg in the refrigerator is hard-boiled, spin it. If it spins on the countertop, it's hard-boiled. If it wobbles around, it's raw.
- Eggs at room temperature beat up fluffier.
- For easy removal of shells from hard-boiled eggs, immerse them in ice-cold water for about 5- 10 minutes before shelling.
- If baked meringue (whipped egg whites) is runny, add 1 teaspoon of cornstarch to the sugar before beating it into the egg whites.
- Before baking your meringue, sprinkle 2 teaspoons of granulated sugar over the top.
    - This make for easier slicing and less tearing of the browned peaks.
- Use medium to large eggs in your recipes. Extra-large eggs may cause a cake to fall somewhat after it has cooled.
- When frying bacon, separate the slices in the package by rolling it up before opening it.
- Bacon won't curl as bad when you fry it if you dip it into cold water first. Don't put it into hot grease.
- Lemons give more juice if they are at room-temperature before slicing.
- Store popcorn in your freezer. Almost every kernel pops!

- If the center of your hamburger is not done, when patting out burger patties, make a hole in the center with your finger. This prevents the "puffy" raw center. If you freeze hamburger patties for later use, make sure to make a hole before freezing.
- Thaw fish in milk for a "fresh fish" taste.
- If creamed-corn is stuck on the bottom of your pan, add water and boil for easy removal. This works well with casserole dishes in the oven, as well.
- Remove lime deposits from pots, tea kettles and coffee pots by cleaning with equal parts vinegar and water.
- Clean silver with a damp cloth and baking soda.
- Old toothbrushes are wonderful kitchen and bathroom helpers in those small. hard-to- reach places. Please clean old brushes thoroughly before using in the kitchen.
- If drain is clogged with grease, pour down a cup each of salt and baking soda followed by a pot of boiling water.
- Keep your septic tank healthy by pouring buttermilk in your drain once a month.
- If your brown sugar has hardened, place a slice of apple in the container.
- Tear less when cutting your onions by working from the top down to the root end.
- Remove the core from a head of lettuce by hitting the core end sharply on the counter.
- Lettuce and celery keep longer in a paper lunch bag instead of the plastic wrap.
- To absorb grease in a pot of homemade soup, drop in a lettuce leaf. It will attract the grease. Dispose of leaf before consuming the soup.
- Drop a few ice cubes in the soup, they will also collect excess grease. Remove them quickly before they melt.
- If you have over-salted soup or veggies, add a few cut-up raw potatoes. They absorb excess salt. Discard the potatoes.
- Adding a teaspoon of sugar and a teaspoon of cider vinegar to over-salted vegetables or soup will also help dilute the salt content.

- If your gravy turns out lumpy, brown the flour well before adding your liquid. Whisk well.
- If you have greasy gravy, add 1/4 teaspoon of baking soda.
- Fresh whipped cream whips up better if you chill the cream, bowl and beaters.
- If you have runny whipped cream, add an egg white and chill. Re-beat and it will fluff up again.
- Add a few drops of lemon juice to whipping cream to make it whip up better.
- Add a few drops of lemon juice to simmering rice to keep the grains separated.
- When sautéing or panfrying, always heat the pan first before adding the oil or butter.
- If your pasta or rice is boiling over, adding 2 teaspoons of butter or oil will prevent this. You can also grease the top couple of inches of your pot before you add water to boil.
- When spooning out shortening, run the spoon under hot water and it will release easily.
- When broiling, add water to the pan section to prevent the grease from burning to the bottom of the pan and for easier clean-up.
- If tomatoes are not ripe enough, put them in a brown lunch bag and close. Keep at room temperature for a few days to hasten ripening.
- Remove skin from tomatoes, peaches, or pears easier by dipping into them boiling water before peeling.
- Oven-baked potatoes bake quicker if you first boil them in salted water for 10 minutes before placing in the pre-heated oven.
- To prevent splattering when pan frying, sprinkle salt in the pan.
- When frying chicken, flour the chicken and then refrigerate it for an hour or so. The coating sticks better.
- When browning meats, make sure the meat is dry and the pan and oil are very hot.

Hot-Soup and Rice

Have you ever wondered why Chinese soups stay hot longer than those you cook at home? The secret is usually in the pepper oil, which makes the soup not only spicy hot but also temperature hot because it acts as an insulator on the surface of the soup. Any edible additive that can insulate the surface of soup will help to keep it hot longer. In addition, ingredients (i.e., solute) that lower the freezing point of soup (as with water) will also lower the cooling point of the soup.

Egg-Washing

Don't egg-wash me, please. Egg wash consists of a mixture of various ingredients that are combined to be brushed on the surface of breads and rolls before baking in order to give the crust an added brownness, crispness and/or sheen after the item is baked. Depending on the ingredients added to the mixture, an egg wash can provide a variety of different appearances to the surface of baked goods. The basic egg wash is a simple mixture of egg and water stirred or beaten together. Milk is also often used for the mixture. Below is a general guide for applying egg wash options:

- Whole egg and salt - provides a shiny surface
- Whole egg and milk - provides a medium shiny surface
- Whole egg and water - provides a golden amber colored surface
- Egg yolk and water - provides a shiny surface with a golden amber color
- Egg yolk and cream - provides a shiny surface with a darker brown color
- Egg white - provides a crispy surface with a lighter coloring

Adaptation of Cooking Tools

From the traditional grinding stones, electric blenders and modern food processors to revolutionary infrared kitchen aids, humans have devised and developed tools dedicated to the pursuit of cooking. Grinding stones have played a special role in the history of mankind. In ancient times, Neolithic and Upper Paleolithic people used millstone to grind grains, nuts, rhizomes and other vegetable food products for consumption. These implements are often called grinding stones. They used either saddlestones or rotary querns turned by hand. Such devices were also used to grind pigments and metal ores prior to smelting. Various uses have been documented over the centuries. Millstones are used in windmills and watermills, including tide mills, for grinding wheat or other grains. In old-time Britain millstones were used for grinding barley. In France, burrstones were used for finer grinding. In India, grinding stones (Chakki) were used to grind grains and spices. These consist of a stationary stone cylinder upon which a smaller stone cylinder rotates. Smaller ones, for household use, were operated by two people. Larger ones, for community or commercial use, used livestock to rotate the upper cylinder.

Until the modern time, grinding stones were a big part of the ethnic kitchens. Women have used it for grinding of grains and spices. There are still some indigenous villagers in some cultures who are still using grinding stones. Expert users claim they like grinding stones because of the preciseness they can get, in spite of the laborious process. To grind, women would use a piece of stone in a cylindrical shape in both hand. She would put grains on the surface of the base stone and would run the smaller stone over the grain using all her might. She would move the implement back and forth across the surface of the grinding until the grains are well grinded to the level of fineness desired. In the Nigerian Yoruba language, the base stone is called "ọlọ," which literally means grinder. The smaller hand stone is called "ọmọ ọlọ," which literally means "child of the grinder." Of course, "mother" and "child" must go together in other to get the grinding job done. Using "child" this way in the Yoruba vernacular makes references to the smaller or lesser member of a partnership or pairing of implements. In our present modern times, technology and science have since changed the way spices and ingredients are manipulated in the kitchen. For example, in Puerto Rico, a caldero, which is practically a Dutch Oven, is used often used for cooking rice. The caldero is the workhorse or centerpiece of Hispanic kitchens due to its versatility and unique design. The caldero ("cauldron" in English) has rounded sides, a tight fitting lid, and superior heat distribution. Calderos are used to cook rice, beans, braise meat, and simmer stews and soups.

Ethnicity and Food Habits

Food habits are greatly influenced by ethnicity. Contrary to how some people view it, ethnicity is not the same as race. Ethnicity refers to the group to which an individual belongs based on cultural affiliation, language, food habits, social interests, religion, and family patterns. Race generally refers to the biological division to which an individual belongs based on color of skin, color and texture of hair, physical features, and other bodily characteristics. Because of intermarriage and evolution of time, race is sometimes viewed as a social construct and not amenable to strict demarcation lines. The lines of food demarcation are very fuzzy. Over the generations, food practices and recipes have cross-fertilized and morphed into hybrids of recipes and customized variations to fit the consumer's tastes and preferences.

Minding the Mind, Body, and Soul

Body and soul benefit from rice products of the ethnic kitchen. Of the body, eating provides nourishments that are essential for life, healing, and thriving as a social being.

Of the soul, eating offers pleasure that excites the senses that makes a person what he or she is spiritually and socially. While the body represents the engagement of time and space, it is the soul that creates the aura that ties everything together. Essentially, the soul is the atmosphere, spiritual or otherwise, within which the body resides.

Of the mind, eating expands the mind both through the anticipatory comfort of the food as well as the gratification of going through the action of consumption. A dull mind can result from not being exposed to a wide variety of food. The quote below summarizes the essentials of culinary physics:

> "...all the charming and beautiful things, from the Song of Songs, to bouillabaisse, and from the nine Beethoven symphonies to the Martini cocktail, have been given to humanity by men who, when the hour came, turned from tap water to something with color in it, and more in it than mere oxygen and hydrogen." - H.L. Mencken

Chapter 7

Popular Rice Recipes

Cooking is about the transformation of food from one form to another form. The components for this transformation are the ingredients contained in a recipe. Transformation in this sense, is as much about science as it is about the art of cooking.

Easy does it. Make it rice and easy. Some people make cooking rice fun and entertaining. Such is the case of my older son, Ibrahim Adetokunboh Kolawole (aka Ade), an Automotive Engineer at General Motors, who, as a demonstration of his love of rice, created a comical home YouTube video of how to cook and enjoy rice. The video link is provided below.
Ibrahim cooks rice.mpeg: https://www.youtube.com/watch?v=DS eZazIT9w.

Other equally hilarious video of cooking rice can be found online. The recipes in this chapter represent a diverse collection from various sources over various cultures and geographical locations around the world. As I have suggested throughout this book, please feel free to experiment with the recipes. If there appears that there is a gap in a particular recipe, simply fill the gap with your own imagination and creative kitchen experimentations. This is how new good recipes are originated!

The joy of home cooking is doing what you please. Cooking, like writing and painting, is an art form. You mix carefully selected ingredients to create exquisite meals. In writing, you select word to compose sentences, which form paragraphs, which are concatenated to form a logical flow of imagination. In painting, carefully selected colors in varying degrees of intensity are amalgamated to form beautiful scenes. In my recipes, the objective is to be creative, innovative, and adaptive. Really, there are few recipe rules. So, don't be timid breaking the rules. Go out on a limb to try something new and do something different. More dynamics to you in your kitchen!

To aid you in translating one recipe measurement into another measurement, the following the conversion factors are provided.

Kitchen Measurement Conversions

A pinch 1/8 ......less than teaspoon

3 teaspoons (tsp) ...1 tablespoon (tbsp)

2 tablespoons.............................1/8 cup

4 tablespoons...............................1/4 cup

16 tablespoons.......................................1cup

5 tbsp. + 1 tsp..1/3 cup

4 ounces (oz)...1/2 cup

8 ounces (oz)..1 cup

16 ounces (oz) ....2 cups.........453 grams......1 pound (lb)

1 ounce...2 tbsp

1 cup of liquid..1/2 pint

2 cups...1 pint

2 pint...1 quart

4 cups of liquid.............................1 quart

4 quarts......................................1gallon

8 quarts...........1 peck (apples, pears, etc.)

1 jigger.............1-1/2 fl ounces (fl oz)

1 jigger................3 tablespoons

VOLUME

Multiply	by	to obtain
acre-foot	1233.5	cubic meters
cubic cm	0.06102	cubic inches
cubic feet	1728	cubic inches
	7.480	gallons (US)
	0.02832	cubic meters
	0.03704	cubic yards
liter	1.057	liquid quarts
	0.908	dry quarts
	61.024	cubic inches
gallons (US)	231	cubic inches
	3.7854	liters
	4	quarts
	0.833	British gallons

	128	U.S. fluid ounces
quarts (US)	0.9463	liters

ENERGY, HEAT POWER

Multiply	by	to obtain
BTU	1055.9	joules
	0.2520	kg-calories
watt-hour	3600	joules
	3.409	BTU
HP (electric)	746	watts
BTU/second	1055.9	watts
watt-second	1.00	joules

WEIGHT

Multiply	by	to obtain
grams	0.03527	ounces
kilograms	2.2046	pounds
ounces	28.350	grams
pound	16	ounces
	453.6	grams
BTU/second	1055.9	watts
watt-second	1.00	joules

TEMPERATURE

Conversion formulas	
Celsius to Kelvin	$K = C + 273.15$
Celsius to Fahrenheit	$F = (9/5)C + 32$
Fahrenheit to Celsius	$C = (5/9)(F - 32)$
Fahrenheit to Kelvin	$K = (5/9)(F + 459.67)$

Fahrenheit to Rankin	R = F + 459.67

PRESSURE

Multiply	by	to obtain
atmospheres	1.01325	bars
	33.90	feet of water
	29.92	inches of mercury
	760.0	mm of mercury
bar	75.01	cm of mercury
	14.50	pounds/sq inch
newtons/sq cm	1.450	pounds/sq inch
pounds/sq inch	0.06805	atmospheres
	2.036	inches of mercury
	27.708	inches of water

Cooking Rice Well

Avoid having your rice too wet or sticky. The best way to achieve this is to leave the rice alone, difficult as this might be. The temptation is to always sneak a peek by opening the rice pot. This is wrong. You must resist this temptation. Just leave the rice alone and let it do its natural magic, if you have followed the recipe directions correctly. I invite and encourage you to experiment with the recipes below and don't be timid in putting your own new twist on the recipes. Enjoy!

Chicken and Rice - Caribbean Style (provided by Maria Miah)

Ingredients
Sofrito:
1 small Yellow Onion, peel, cut into chunks

1 small Green Bell Pepper, cut in half, remove seeds, wash and cut into chunks
1 small bunch of fresh cilantro, wash, cut off half of the stems
1 small head of garlic, peel
½-1 cup of water

1/3 cup vegetable oil
4 small whole bay leaves
Salt to taste
Fresh ground pepper to taste
2 tablespoons of Tomato Paste
2 tablespoons of Alcaparado (olives and capers) or chopped stuffed Spanish Olives (optional)
2 envelopes of Sason powder (Goya product)
1 envelope or 2 boullion cubes of Chicken broth concentrate
5 cups of water
4 large boneless chicken breasts, washed, cut into cubes or strips
4 cups Jasmine Rice

Directions
Prepare Sofrito (Caribbean starter seasoning):

After washing, cutting, peeling, and deseeding all of the sofrito ingredients, place in a blender with a bit of the water and blend until pureed. Blend all ingredients, mix thoroughly and place in a container.

- On medium high, heat the 1/3 cup vegetable oil in a medium stainless-steel pot or aluminum rice pot.

- When oil is hot add the bay leaves, once the leaves turn dark add the chicken pieces and sauté until cooked through.

- Move the cooked chicken pieces to the side of the pot. Add 5 tablespoons of the prepared sofrito to the pot (place the remaining sofrito in the freezer for future use. It will last up to 6 months in the freezer).

- Add the tomato paste, alcaparado or Spanish Olives, Sason Powder and the chicken broth concentrate to the sofrito, stir together and allow a minute to fry before mixing everything together; lower the heat to medium.

- Add the 5 cups of water, stir thoroughly and allow to come to a slow boil. Add salt and pepper to taste.

- While the chicken mixture is at a slow boil, wash the rice three times or until liquid is clear from the white residue.

- Add the rice to the liquid, mix thoroughly and allow the liquid to evaporate. Once the liquid has evaporated, stir the rice thoroughly, lower the heat to low and cover.

- Cook covered rice for 30 minutes. Uncover and stir to move the uncooked rice on top to the bottom, cover and steam for another 15 minutes. Serves 8.

Perfect Steamed Jasmine Rice
(provided by Maria Miah)

<u>Ingredients</u>
4 cups of quality Jasmine Rice
6 cups of water
3 tablespoons of vegetable or canola oil
½ teaspoon of salt

<u>Directions</u>
In a deep stainless steel pot or aluminum rice pot place the 6 cups of water, oil and salt and allow the water to reach rolling boil over high heat.

Using cool water, wash the rice three times or more until the water runs clear of the white residue.

Place rice in the boiling water and lower to medium heat, stir the rice thoroughly and allow the water to evaporate completely.

Once the water has evaporated, stir and break up the rice thoroughly, lower the heat to a very low flame, cover with lid and steam for 25 minutes.

After 25 minutes, uncover the rice and stir the rice to loosen and to move any uncooked rice to the bottom of the pot. Cover the rice and continue steaming for another 15 minutes or until desired tenderness. Serves 6.

Rice with Vienna Sausage
(provided by Maria Miah)

<u>Ingredients</u>
Sofrito:

1 small Yellow Onion, peel, cut into chunks

1 small Green Bell Pepper, cut in half, remove seeds, wash and cut into chunks

1 small bunch of fresh cilantro, wash, cut off half of the stems

1 small head of garlic, peel

½-1 cup of water

1/3 cup vegetable oil

4 small whole bay leaves

Salt to taste

Fresh ground pepper to taste

2 tablespoons of Tomato Paste

2 tablespoons of Alcaparado (olives and capers) or chopped stuffed Spanish Olives (optional)

2 envelopes of Sason powder (Goya product)

1 envelope or 2 boullion cubes of Chicken broth concentrate

5 cups of water

3 small cans (4.6 oz) or 1 large can (8 oz.) can of Vienna Sausage

4 cups Jasmine Rice

Instructions

Prepare Sofrito (Caribbean starter seasoning):

After washing, cutting, peeling, and deseeding all of the sofrito ingredients, place in a blender with a bit of the water and blend until pureed. Blend all ingredients, mix thoroughly and place in a container.

- On medium high, heat the 1/3 cup vegetable oil in a medium stainless-steel pot or aluminum rice pot.

- When oil is hot add the bay leaves, once the leaves turn dark add the Vienna sausage and sauté until slightly browned.

- Move the Vienna sausage to the side of the pot. Add 5 tablespoons of the prepared sofrito to the pot (place the remaining sofrito in the freezer for future use. It will last up to 6 months in the freezer).

- Add the tomato paste, alcaparado or Spanish Olives, Sason Powder and the chicken broth concentrate to the sofrito, stir together and allow a minute to fry before mixing everything together; lower the heat to medium.

- Add the 5 cups of water, stir thoroughly and allow to come to a slow boil. Add salt and pepper to taste.

- While the mixture is at a slow boil, wash the rice three times or more in cool water until liquid is clear from the white residue.

- Add the rice to the liquid, mix thoroughly and allow the liquid to evaporate. Once the liquid has evaporated, stir the rice thoroughly, lower the heat to low and cover.

- Cook covered rice for 30 minutes. Uncover and stir to move the uncooked rice on top to the bottom, cover and steam for another 15 minutes. Serves 8.

Baked Rice Pudding
(Provided by Deb Donley)

Baking this dessert instead of cooking on the stove makes this rice pudding a wonderful custardy rich dessert.

Ingredients
- 4 eggs, beaten
- 3 cups milk
- 1 cup sugar
- ½ teaspoon salt

- 2 teaspoons vanilla
- 2 cups cooked rice
- ½ teaspoon cinnamon
- ½ cup raisins

Instructions
1. Beat eggs. Stir in sugar. Stir in remaining ingredients.
2. Spray casserole dish with vegetable oil spray. Pour mixture into dish.
3. Set dish in pan of hot water and bake at 300 degrees for 90 minutes.
4. After first 30 minutes of cooking, insert spoon at edge of pudding and stir from the bottom to distribute rice and raisins.

Isi Garlic Rice
(adapted from Isi Cookbook by Iswat and Deji Badiru)

Ingredients
1 tsp butter
1 tsp olive oil
4 cloves garlic, minced
¾ cup uncooked jasmine rice
1-1/2 cups chicken broth
Sea salt and white pepper (add to taste preference)
1 tbsp fresh parsley, chopped

Directions
Heat the butter and olive oil in a saucepan over medium heat. Add the minced garlic and cook, stirring constantly, for one minute. Add the rice and cook for 3-4 minutes, stirring often to avoid the rice sticking to the pan. Add the chicken broth and season with sea salt and white pepper (to taste). Bring to a boil. Reduce heat to medium low. Cover and let cook for 20 minutes. Remove the rice from the burner without removing the lid and let it sit (or rest) for 5 minutes.

Carefully remove the lid and fluff the rice with a fork. Sprinkle with chopped parsley and serve fresh.

Deji's Rice with Roasted Corn and Black Beans

Experimentation and adaptation are the boon of enjoying rice in all its glorious flavors. The recipe below is my own adaptation of a recipe that was originally based on quinoa, a fiber-rich grain from South America.

Ingredients
3 cups of cooked white rice
2 cups of frozen corn, thawed
1 cup quartered grape tomatoes
1 cup cooked black beans, rinsed and drained
1 cup chopped green onions
¼ cup and 1 tbls canola oil
2 tsp fresh lime juice
½ tsp lime zest
1 tsp coarse salt
½ tsp sugar
½ tsp ground cumin
¼ tsp black pepper

Directions
1. With cooked rice ready in a large bowl, heat ¼ cup oil in large skillet over medium heat. Add corn. Cook and stir for 10 minutes or until corn is slightly browned and tender.
2. Stir in 2/3 cup of green onions and coarse salt. Cook for 2 minutes. Gently stir in tomatoes and black beans. Warm briefly. Add corn mixture to rice.
3. Combine lime juice, lime zest, sugar, cumin and black pepper in a small bowl. Whisk in 1 tablespoon of oil until blended. Pour over rice mixture. Toss to coat. Sprinkle with remaining green onions.

4. Serve warm or chilled with roasted chicken or grilled fish for even more protein.

ENJOY and experiment more!

White rice with pinto beans
(provided by Ginger Swire-Clark and Elsa Swire)

Instructions for Basic White Rice

Use 2 Qt microwavable dish (Corning or Pyrex work well). Mix 1 cup white rice with 1 1/2 cups water. Add 1/2 tsp salt and 1/2 tsp onion powder plus 2 tsp olive oil. Mix all ingredients, cover with lid, and cook in microwave 5 min on HIGH (until water boils). Stir gently, cover with lid, then cook in microwave ~ 16 min on level 4 (LOW; slower cooking until water is absorbed).

Remove from microwave and stir, leave covered until ready to serve.

This recipe could be adapted to be stovetop, but one must be careful to continue stirring the rice to keep it from burning or sticking to the bottom of a dish.

Ingredients for Pinto Beans

1 Tbsp olive oil
1 Tbsp Sofrito (by Goya)
1 Tbsp Recaíto (by Goya)
1/4 ham bouillon cube
Sprinkle of Sazon
 Cilantro (1/4 clump + a couple of sprigs)
16oz can pinto beans (Bush's Best)

Instructions

In 2 Qt or 3 Qt non-stick pot, add 1 Tbsp olive oil, 1 Tbsp Sofrito (Goya), 1 Tbsp Recaíto (Goya), 1/4 ham bouillon cube, "dash" of Sazon, a couple of sprigs of cilantro. Sauteé on stovetop - medium heat for around 1-2 min.

Add entire can of Pinto Beans including liquid (we use Bush's Best Pinto Beans). Take the empty can and fill ~ 1/3 with water. Swirl can and then add the additional water to the pot. Stir gently.

Cover with lid and increase heat to HIGH. Once beans reach a boil, oil for around 5 minutes. Stir gently and add ~ 1/4 "clump" of washed cilantro (add more if you like, can add less as well; leave the stems on the cilantro and do not tear or chop). Cover with lid and reduce heat to LOW, so that beans will simmer. The pot can be left covered at this temperature until the beans are ready to serve. Prior to serving, the cilantro can be carefully removed.

Arroz con gandules (Rice with Pigeon Peas) and AJI-LI-MOJILI (pronounced Ah-Hee-Lee-Moh-Hee-Lee)
(provided by Ginger Swire-Clark and Elsa Swire)

Ingredients
Arroz con gandules
1 tsp olive oil
2 Tbsp Sofrito (by Goya)
1/4 cube ham bouillon
Sprinkle of Sazón
Sprigs of Cilantro
1 cup white rice
1 can Goya Green Pigeon Peas (Gandules Verdes)
1 1/3 cups liquid
1/4 tsp salt
1/4 tsp onion powder

Instructions
Use Corning 2 Qt casserole dish. Sauteé sofrito, bouillon, sprigs of cilantro in olive oil by adding to dish and microwaving (covered) on HIGH for 1 min. Drain can of gandules and reserve the liquid in a 2 cup pyrex. Add rice to the sautéed sofrito mixture and blend.

Take the liquid from the can of gandules and add enough water to equal 1 1/3 cups then add this to the rice. Sprinkle salt and onion power and stir gently. Cover and cook in microwave on HIGH for 5 min. Remove from microwave, add the gandules and stir gently. Cover and continue to cook in microwave for 15-16 min on setting 4 (LOW). Stir and let cool a bit before service

Pork with arroz con gandules is a traditional Christmas meal in Puerto Rico. It is served by itself or with a dressing called AJI-LI-MOJILI, which is used on both the pork and on the arroz con gandules

AJI-LI-MOJILI (pronounced Ah-Hee-Lee-Moh-Hee-Lee)
(provided by Ginger Swire-Clark and Elsa Swire)

Ingredients
2 large cloves of garlic (run through a garlic press)
1/8 tsp ground black pepper
1/4 cup olive oil
2 Tbsp lemon juice (can be fresh or bottled)
1 tsp salt
2 Tbsp red wine vinegar

Instructions
Mix ingredients in the order given in cruet (something that can be sealed and shaken). Can be kept at room temp for a few hours after mixing and then any remaining aji-li-mojili should be refrigerated. Aji-li-mójili should be served at room temp or slightly warmer. Aji-li-mójili is delicious on pork and fish

Asopao (chicken and rice soup; pronounced Ah-soh-pah-oh)
(provided by Ginger Swire-Clark and Elsa Swire)

Note: This recipe is a bit harder to articulate because how to make it depends on the preferences of the cook and eaters. This is the basic recipe. It can be tweaked to specific preferences.

Ingredients
2 large boneless chicken breasts or 1 package of chicken tenderloins, cut into bite-sized pieces (around 3/4")
Adobo or Adobo light
Onion Powder
Garlic Powder
2 Tbsp Sofrito
1-2 Tbsp Olive oil
Chicken bouillon cube(s) (one bouillon cube per 4-6 cups water)
Whole Green olives with pimento (these will need to be sliced in half so that the olive halves keep the pimento inside; approx 8-10 whole olives per large chicken breast)
White rice (~ 1/4 cup rice per large chicken breast or ~ 3/4 cup total per package of chicken tenderloins)
Cilantro

Instructions
Cut the chicken breasts (or chicken tenderloins) into bite-sized pieces with cooking scissors/kitchen shears
Season the chicken pieces with Adobo, onion powder, and garlic powder. (Regular adobo contains salt, so be careful not to over-season)

Heat nonstick pot on medium to medium-high heat then sauteé olive oil and Sofrito. After ~ 1 minute to sautee the olive oil and Sofrito, add the seasoned chicken. Stir the olive oil/Sofrito and the chicken together. Cook the chicken for 4-6 minutes, stirring and turning often to make sure the chicken and sofrito do not burn.

Turn down the heat if it is splattering or if the sofrito appears to be burning/caramelizing. Once the chicken is cooked through (no pink in the middle), add 4-6 cups very hot water and cube of chicken bouillon. Add rice, then stir. Cover with lid and increase to HIGH until boiling. Allow to boil for 5 minutes, then turn the temperature down to Simmer/LOW. It may be necessary to remove the pot from the burner for 2-3 minutes until the burner temperature cools down a bit. Add 1/4-1/2 clump of washed cilantro and the olives w/pimentos. Replace lid and let simmer for ~ 15-20 min, until rice is cooked through.

Remove cilantro before serving.

Additional notes: Asopao can be prepared many different ways. For those who prefer a "soupier" consistency, add more water. Add one additional chicken bouillon cube and 1-2 more tbsp of Sofrito when the cilantro is added if 6+ cups of water are used for a soupier consistency. If a more "stew-like" consistence is preferred, do not add extra water. The recipe can be scaled up proportionately and one would need to use a larger non-stick pot. Leftovers can be refrigerated.

Wild Rice Salad with Cashews

Rice is good. Cashews are good. Salad is definitely good and desirable. Why not combine all three for a really healthy meal? The recipe below does just that:

Ingredients:
1 cup uncooked wild rice
4 cups chicken broth
3 tablespoons of olive oil
1½ cup cashews, coarsely chopped
2 green onions, sliced

Dressing:
3 tablespoons of seasoned rice vinegar or apple cider vinegar
2 tablespoons of olive oil
1 tablespoons Asian sesame oil
1 clove garlic, minced
¼ tablespoon salt
A dash of freshly ground pepper

Instructions:
1. In a strainer, rinse wild rice under cool running water. Drain well.
2. In a 3-quart saucepan, bring rice and chicken broth to a boil over high heat
3. Reduce heat and simmer, covered, for 45 minutes or until rice is tender. Drain excess liquid and set rice aside.
4. In a medium skillet, heat 3 tablespoons oil over medium heat. Add peppers and cook for 5 minutes or until tender.
5. Add cashews and green onions. Cook for 2 to 3 minutes or until nuts begin to brown. Remove from heat. In a large bowl, stir wild rice with bell pepper mixture.
6. For dressing, combine vinegar, oils, garlic, salt, and pepper in a jar with a tight-fitting lid. Shake well. Pour dressing over salad and toss to coat the salad. Cover and refrigerate for at least two hours.
7. Enjoy!

Puerto Rican Rice and Pigeon Peas

Ingredients
1 tbsp. extra virgin olive oil
¼ lb. country ham, cubed
½ green bell pepper, chopped (about ½ cup)
½ yellow onion, chopped (about ½ cup)
2 packets sazon with coriander and annatto
1 tbsp. minced garlic

2 tsp. finely chopped fresh cilantro
1 tsp. oregano
1½ cups medium grain rice
1 can (15 oz.) green pigeon peas
4 oz. tomato sauce
1/4 cup Manzanillas Olives Stuffed with Minced Pimientos, sliced

Directions
Heat oil in a medium, heavy saucepan over medium-high heat. Add ham to pan; cook until brown, about 5 minutes. Stir in peppers and onions; cook, stirring occasionally, scraping up brown bits from bottom, until vegetables are soft and translucent, 10 minutes. Add sazón, garlic, cilantro and oregano. Cook until fragrant, about 30 seconds.

Add rice to pan. Cook, stirring frequently, until coated in oil and toasted, about 1 minute. Stir in pigeon peas, tomato sauce, olives and 1½ cups water; using a wooden spoon, stir once and bring rice mixture to a boil. Cook, uncovered, until water is evaporated, about 10 minutes. Gently stir rice from bottom up.

Lower heat to medium low and cook, covered, until rice is tender, about 15 minutes. Remove saucepan from heat. Gently fluff rice with fork. Cover pan and let stand 5 minutes.

Puerto Rican-style Yellow Rice (Arroz Amarillo)

Ingredients
1 Tbsp. olive oil
⅛ tsp. Yellow Food Coloring
¼ tsp. Adobo con Pimiento (With Pepper)
1 packet Sazón with Coriander and Annatto
1 packet Chicken Bouillon
1 Tbsp. Frozen Recaito, thawed

½ Cup tomato sauce

2 Cups water

2 Cups medium-grain white rice

1 Tbsp. diced ham

2 Tbsp. alcaparrado

Instructions

Heat olive oil over medium heat.

Add the next 7 ingredients.

When the water comes to a boil, add the rice.

Turn the heat down to low.

When the water has evaporated until it is level with the rice, add the ham and alcaparrado, stir once, put the lid on and turn heat as low as possible.

Let rice simmer approximately 20 minutes. Makes six servings.

Hawaiian Pineapple Rice

Ingredients

3⁄4 cup cooked chicken, diced

1 egg

2 cups cooked rice, cold

2 green onions, diced

1⁄4 cup carrot, finely diced

1⁄4 cup pineapple, drained and diced

2 tablespoons soy sauce

1 teaspoon sesame oil

2 tablespoons vegetable oil

pepper

Directions

Heat oil, and add the chicken, rice, onions, carrots, soy sauce and sesame oil.

Stir-fry until hot (about 2 minutes).

Add the egg and continue stirring while cooking adding pepper to taste.

Add pineapple to warm rice and serve.

Note: Always use cold cooked rice for stir fry, it's the secret.

Hawaiian Pineapple Coconut Cashew Rice

Ingredients

1 1/2 cups uncooked long grained rice, rinsed and drained

1 20 oz. can crushed pineapple chunks in pineapple juice (not syrup)

1 13.5 oz. can unsweetened coconut milk

3 tablespoons sweetened coconut flakes

1 tablespoon Thai red curry paste

1 teaspoon garlic powder

1/2 teaspoon onion powder

1/2 teaspoon ground ginger

1/2 teaspoon salt

1/8 teaspoon pepper

Garnish

3 tablespoons lime juice, more or less to taste

1/2 cup salted roasted cashews

1/2 cup chopped cilantro

freshly cracked salt and pepper to taste

Instructions

Drain pineapple juice from crushed pineapple in a measuring cup. Add coconut milk to equal 3 cups liquid, adding water if necessary.

Add liquid to a large pan and bring to a gentle simmer then stir in all remaining ingredients except Garnishes. Bring to a boil then cover and reduce heat to low (dial should be a little above lowest setting). Simmer for approximately 20 minutes or until rice is tender, stirring at 15 minutes, adding water if necessary.

When rice is tender, remove from heat and let rest 5 minutes, covered.

When ready to serve (not before), stir in lime juice, cilantro and cashews.

Taste and season with freshly cracked salt and pepper and additional lime juice to taste if desired.

Hawaiian Luau Rice

Ingredients
basmati rice - 2 cups
water - 2 cups
coconut oil - 2-3 tablespoons (your rice will really soak up the coconut oil quickly so use a non-stick pan)
onion - 1 small chopped or about 1/2 cup
ginger - 1 teaspoon
garlic - 2 cloves chopped
ham - 1/2 cup sliced thinly (I used deli ham but you can exchange with spam or fresh ham)
desiccated coconut - 1/2 cup shredded (Can use fresh coconut shredded)
chicken powder (gluten free) - 1-2 teaspoons to taste (this is chicken bouillon in the powdered form) - you can also use chicken bouillon cubes and just crush into a powder and you can add to taste.
white pepper - 1/4 teaspoon or to taste
pineapple - 1 cup chopped fresh (can exchange with canned)
macadamia nuts - crushed garnish optional for the topping
green onions - 2 tablespoons chopped for garnish

Instructions
Step 0: The day or two before, wash your rice thoroughly add 2 cups of rice and 2 cups of water to your pan and cook on stove top or steamer. Allow rice to completely cool and place in the refrigerator overnight.

Step 1: Toast your coconut in a non-stick skillet until it is toasty brown. Set aside.

Step 2: Place your coconut oil, onions, garlic, ginger in the pan until aromatic. Add the ham and cook quickly until lightly golden.

Step 3: Add your cooked basmati rice, chicken powder and white pepper and mix quickly in your pan until all of the rice is covered evenly with the coconut oil and seasoning. Add the pineapple, green onions and toasted coconut back into the pan and continue stirring quickly, just until warmed. Reserve a little toasted coconut on the side for garnishing.

Step 4: Serve on plate and garnish with toasted crushed macadamia nuts, toasted coconut and green onions.

Cambodian Beef Fried Rice

Ingredients
- 500 g rice
- 200 g butter
- 500 g tomatoes
- 200 g onion
- 300 g salad
- 200 g cooking oil
- 100 g garlic
- salt to taste
- 4-5 teaspoons fish sauce
- 4-5 teaspoons soya sauce
- 4-5 teaspoons vinegar
- 500g beef

Preparation

Slice beef into pieces. Chop the radish, garlic, and onions into small pieces separately. Cook the rice. Add cooking oil to a frypan and brown the garlic. Remove the garlic, add the beef and cook until well-done. Then add tomatoes, chopped onions, sugar, salt, soy sauce and cook until tomatoes breaking easily. Add rice and mix until well cooked. Serve immediately with salad. Makes four servings.

French Rolled Rice with Tuna

<u>Ingredients</u>
- 300 g Camargue long rice
- crab meat
- 200 g fresh tuna fillet cut into thin slices
- 4 rice wrappers (made from rice flour, about 30 cm in diameter)
- 5 cc of cream
- 8 tomatoes, sliced
- 1 pinch of five-spices, 1 curry leaf
- 1 carrot, 1 tender courgette (French Zucchini), 1 fennel
- 3 sticks/sprigs of chervil
- Dressing made with lemon juice, fine salt, ground pepper, olive oil

<u>Preparation</u>
Cook the rice in salted, boiling water for 8 to 10 minutes. Mix the rice with the crab meat, tomatoes, cream, a few drops of lemon dressing and the spices. Spread out the tuna slices and sprinkle with lemon dressing to marinate. Soak the rice wrappers in cold water for 5 minutes, drain off the water on a piece of linen, then cut the wrappers into four pieces. On each piece, spread tuna slices and three tablespoons of rice mixture and then roll. Grate the vegetables finely using a vegetable grater, put dressing on them and add the olive oil and a drop of lemon. Place vegetable salad in the center of the plates, arrange the rolls of rice around it and decorate with sprigs of chervil. Sprinkle with vinaigrette. Makes six servings.

Gambian Chuyi Dewtir

Ingredients
- 1 kg of fish
- half litre of palm oil
- 0.5 kg of rice
- 3 tablespoons of tomato puree
- 250 g of sliced onions
- 125 g of tomato concasse
- half litre of fish stock or water
- half teaspoon of cayenne pepper
- seasoning
- leaf spinach

Preparation
Cut fish into strips, wash and drain. Heat the heat palm oil in saucepan, fry the fish, remove and keep warm. Fry onions, add tomato puree and cook. Add the concasse and cayenne pepper, stirring well. Then add the fish stock (or water) and seasoning and boil for 15 minutes. Add spinach and boil for 5 minutes, reduce heat and simmer for 1 hour. Serve with boiled rice and garnish with boiled vegetables e.g. pumpkins, cassava, yam, bitter tomato and/or eggplant. Makes four servings.

Kuwait Rice with Shrimps (Morabian)

Ingredients
- 0.5 kg shrimps (peeled)
- 2 cups rice
- 2 tablespoons mixed spices
- 2 chopped onions
- 0.5 cup lentils
- 2 tablespoons chopped coriander

Preparation

Fry prawns with spices, add chopped onion, mix rice with lentils. Cook together in boiling water, serve rice with shrimp mixture on top.

Laos Stir Fried Chicken with Mushrooms

Ingredients
- 6 dried Chinese mushrooms
- 1 small roasting chicken
- 4 cloves garlic, crushed
- half teaspoon finely grated fresh ginger
- 2 tablespoons oil
- 250 ml water
- 2 teaspoons sugar
- 2 tablespoons chopped fresh coriander leaves

Preparation

Soak mushrooms in hot water for 30 minutes. Squeeze dry, remove and discard stems. Cut mushroom caps into quarters if they are large. Cut chicken into small pieces, chopping through the bones. Fry the garlic and ginger in the hot oil for a few seconds, then add chicken and stir fry until its color changes. Add mushrooms, water and sugar, cover and simmer until the chicken is cooked. Sprinkle with chopped coriander and serve with rice. Makes five to six servings.

Madagascar Rice with Ox and Greens

Ingredients
- 500 g chopped ox meat
- 500 g green leaves or edible hearts of plants: a mixture of spinaches, cress, anamamy (solanaceous), anamalao, anatsonga (cruciferous). They may be substituted with Chinese cabbage and salad greens.
- 500 g rice
- 1 onion, chopped

- 3 cloves of garlic, chopped
- 2 tomatoes, chopped
- 50g ginger, sliced
- Salt, black pepper

Preparation

Brown the meat in a cooking pot with a little oil, then add the onions, garlic, and ginger. Add the clean and thinly cut green leaves, tomatoes, 1 cup water, salt and pepper to taste. Bring to a boil for approximately 10 to 15 minutes. Add the rice and additional water. Cover the pot and continue cooking for approximately 15 to 20 minutes.

Suggestion: Serve this dish with sausages and sprinkle it with a some hot chili pepper. Makes four servings.

Pakistani Mutton Biryani

Ingredients
- 1 kg mutton
- 1 kg Basmati rice
- 100 gram yogurt
- salt to taste
- 50 g onion
- 10 g garlic
- 15 g ginger paste
- 5 g cardamom
- 15 g garlic paste
- 5 g cloves
- 250 gm oil or ghee
- few drops kewrra essence
- 0.5 g yellow food color
- 0.5 g sugar

Preparation

Wash and soak the rice in water for 30 to 60 minutes. Boil the rice till it is half cooked, then drain keep it aside. Add mutton, salt and garlic cloves in a pot with 500ml of water. Cook on a low flame till the meat is tender and the water almost evaporates. Slice the onion and fry in about 75 g of oil until light brown. Add the rest of the spices, yogurt and fry for a short time. Add the cooked meat to the fried onions and cook uncovered for a few minutes to evaporate excess water. When most of the water has evaporated, transfer a little rice to a pot, and on top of that add some of the meat/masala mixture. Make layers using half of the rice in and all the meat/masala, then top that off with the remaining rice. Sprinkle over a solution of kewrra, yellow food color and pinch of sugar. Keep the pot tightly closed and simmer over a low flame to steam cook the rice. Serve with salad or garlic chutney.

Senegalese Rice Fish

Ingredients
- 1 kg rice (preferably broken)
- 1 kg fish (preferably one big codfish)
- 250 g tomato puree
- 75 g dried fish
- 2 onions
- Vegetables: carrot, cabbage, yam, okras, eggplants, turnips, fresh tomatoes, fresh hot-peppers, tamarind fruits, parsley, garlic
- Bissap leaves, salt, cooking oil

Preparation

Dice the onions, wash and chop the vegetables. Prepare and clean the fresh fish. Roll the dried fish in the bissap leaves and tie with a string.

Put cooking oil in a pot and heat until it is very hot. Add the diced onion and cook for 1 minute. Stir in the parsley and garlic, then season with salt and pepper. Stuff the cooked mixture inside the fish.

Fry the fish gently in cooking oil for 15 minutes. Add the tomato puree, stirring occasionally for 5 minutes, then add the remaining vegetables. Add water and boil for another 3 minutes. Remove the fish and the vegetables and place them on a plate. Add the rolled dry fish to the pot and cook for another 15 minutes.

Wash and rinse the rice well, place it in another pot, add water and stir once. Cover the pot and cook over a low fire until all the water is absorbed (about 15 to 18 minutes). Do not remove the cover before the end of cooking.

Serving: Place the fish and vegetable at the center of a large plate or tray. Put the cooked rice around the fish. Pour the tomato sauce with the rolled dry fish over the rice. Makes six servings.

Sierra Leone Jollof Rice

Ingredients
- 5 cups of rice
- onions
- 1.3 kg of meat
- 1 piece chicken
- 3 tins of tomato paste
- 1 liter of groundnut oil
- Season vegetables
- 6 beef cubes
- salt and pepper to taste
- seed tomatoes
- bay leaves

Preparation

Stew

Season the chicken and meat. Pour the oil into an empty pot and heat for 5 minutes. Add the chicken and meat, and deep-fry, then set aside. Blend the pepper, onions and seed tomatoes, then fry with the soup cubes. Add the fried chicken, meat and a small amount of water, season, and add salt to taste. Cook until all the water is absorbed, then set aside to cool.

Rice

Wash the rice, season and leave until all water is absorbed. Boil water with small quantity of stew. Pour in rice, tomato paste, bay leaves and salt, cook until all water is absorbed. Serve the rice and stew separately, with boiled vegetables (cabbage, carrot, peas). Makes ten servings.

Nigerian Jollof Rice

Ingredients
5 cups Rice
1 15oz. can tomato sauce
2 large fresh tomatoes
1 6oz. can tomato paste
1 medium onion
2 habanera peppers (hot, adjust to taste)
2 red bell peppers
Garlic to taste
4 maggi or knorr cubes
Curry powder to taste
Ground thyme to taste
5 pieces bay leaves
½ -1 cup of oil
Water

Salt to taste

Directions

- Blend tomato sauce, fresh tomatoes, paste, onion, garlic, habanera peppers, and red bell peppers together. Add very little water as needed during blending for the blade to rotate.
- Pour blended tomato/pepper mixture into a deep cooking pot; add maggi or knorr cubes, thyme, curry; six (6) cups of water, stir and cook for 15 minutes at medium heat.
- Reduce heat to low heat; wash rice and rinse to remove excess starch; add rice to tomato/pepper mixture; stir thoroughly; add oil, bay leaves; mix and cover; steam until all the liquid is absorbed into the rice; then open and stir thoroughly. Add water if needed for softer rice; but too much water, the rice will be mushy or soggy.
- Add salt if needed and simmer for 5 - 10 minutes.

Serve with: Dodo, Moin-Moin, any green vegetables.
Meat: Baked Chicken, Fried Chicken, Baked Fish, Fried Fish or Steak.
Serves ten.

South African Rice Pilau

Ingredients

- 500 g meat, boiled
- 500 g rice - preferably Thai or Basmati
- 1 big onion
- 120mls cooking oil
- 5 cloves of garlic- crushed
- pinch of turmeric (for colour, optional)
- ginger, crushed
- salt to taste
- chili
- 4 sticks cinnamon
- 10 pods of cardamon
- 1 teaspoon of black
- 1 teaspoon of cumin seeds
- 5 buds of cloves

Directions

Heat the spices - cinnamon, cardamon, peppercorns and cumin - for 4 minutes, turning constantly. Then grind to powder. In a pot with a thick base, fry onion, cloves then garlic then ginger at moderate temperature until golden brown. Add the spice powder for two minutes, then add the boiled meat for one minute. Add the rice, stir, then add about two cups of boiling water, salt to taste and turmeric. Mix gently. Repeat the mixing after five minutes. Once water has evaporated and the rice is soft, lower temperature and cover pot. (If rice is not ready add boiling water with a bit of salt around the inside of the pot and turn rice gently.) Serve as a main meal with a salad of tomatoes and onions mixed with a few drops of lemon.

Thailand Seafood Rice Porridge

<u>Ingredients</u>
- 1 kg any selection of fish, prawns, squids, mussels or shell fish
- 1 cup rice
- 6-8 cups water
- 1 clove garlic, crushed
- 1 whole coriander root
- 1 tablespoon salt
- 1 tablespoon pepper corns
- 1 tablespoon vinegar
- 1 celery stalk
- quarter cup chopped garlic
- quarter cup vegetable oil
- 1 tablespoon chopped celery
- 1 tablespoon chopped spring onion
- 1 tablespoon chopped coriander leaves
- 10 sweet basil leaves
- Lime juice, fish sauce and chili to taste

<u>Directions</u>
Wash and prepare all the seafood. Heat the water in a saucepan. Add 1 whole coriander root, crushed garlic, celery stalk, vinegar, salt and pepper corns. Bring to boil. Blanch the seafood in the boiling stock. Reserve the meat and discard the shells or bones. Next, strain the stock into another saucepan. Heat the oil in a frying pan. Fry the chopped garlic and rice. Season with fish sauce. Then pour plenty of the stock into the rice. Bring to boil and simmer for 20-30 minutes. Add the reserved seafood. Sprinkle with the chopped herbs. Serve hot.

Turkish Veiled Pilaf

<u>Ingredients</u>
- 750 g chicken
- 1 cup water
- 1 teaspoon salt
- 2 tablespoon pine nuts
- one-third cup blanched almonds
- quarter cup butter or margarine
- 360 g rice
- 800 g water or broth
- 2 teaspoons salt
- 2 tablespoons currants
- 2 teaspoons black pepper
- 150 g all-purpose flour
- 1 medium-size egg
- half teaspoon salt
- 1 teaspoon oil
- 1 tablespoon water

<u>Directions</u>
Simmer chicken in salted water for 35 minutes or until tender. Remove and drain. Bone, cut into 1 to 1.5 cm cubes and set aside. Set aside 800 g of broth. Fry the pine nuts and almonds in margarine until light golden, reserving 2 teaspoons of margarine to grease casserole. Stir in rice, mixing well. Sauté for a few minutes. Add the hot broth and stir. Sprinkle currants over the rice, cover and simmer for 15 - 20 minutes or until the rice is tender; drain. Remove from heat. Sprinkle with black pepper. Let stand covered for 20 minutes. Sift flour in a bowl and make a hole in center. Add egg, salt, oil and water, blending thoroughly into medium soft dough. Shape into a ball and roll into a pastry layer 1 mm thick. Grease a round casserole 20 - 25 cm in diameter. Line casserole with pastry, leaving overhang, and spoon pilaf and chicken meat into casserole in layers, pressing slightly. Fold edges of pastry over pilaf. Bake in a moderate oven for 15 minutes or

until pastry is light golden. Turn upside down on a serving plate and cut into wedges before serving. Makes six servings.

Nigerian Baked Rice

Ingredients
5 cups uncooked rice
8 cups of water
1 small onion – finely chopped
¼ cup celery – finely chopped
¼ cup finely chopped green and red bell peppers
¼ cup olive oil or butter
½ teaspoon garlic powder
Salt to taste

Direction
- In a deep cooking pot add oil or butter; add rice and stir fry until golden brown (stir constantly to avoid burning); add eight (8) cups of water to per-boil rice for about ten (10) minutes.
- Turn the heat off; add chopped onion, celery, bell peppers and garlic powder; stir and add salt to taste.
- Pour rice into a 9 X 13-inch baking dish; cover with foil; bake at 350 degrees for fifty (50) minutes or until rice is cooked.
- Add more water for softer rice.

Serve with baked chicken, fish or steak.
Serves up to ten.

Nigerian Coconut Rice

Ingredients
4 cups of Rice
6 cups coconut milk

1 lb. boneless chicken - diced

1 lb. shrimp

1 tablespoon ground crayfish or to taste

1 large red bell peppers – diced

1 large fresh tomatoes – diced

½ tablespoon ground pepper or to taste

1 large carrots - diced

1 medium onion - chopped

1/4 cup oil

4 maggi or knorr cubes

Water

Salt to taste

Directions

Step 1.

- Boil chicken with onion and some maggi until tender, cool then dice. Thaw shrimp, drain and set aside.
- Using fresh coconut fruit: crack 3 coconuts open; remove the white flesh and roughly grate;
- Pour hot water to cover grated coconut and leave to stand for about 30 minutes.
- Remove the roughage by press and squeeze the flesh to extract the milk; then sieve the liquid to remove any leftover roughage. The more water, the thinner the milk will be. In general, one fresh coconut will yield about 2 cups of milk **or** use two cans of coconut milk.
- Boil coconut milk for about ten (10) minutes at medium heat; add rice and cook until almost done.
- Add chicken, tomatoes, pepper, maggi or knorr and oil; stir and reduce heat to low, cover and simmer until rice is done and the liquid is absorbed. However, if water is needed add little by little. Do not add too much water or the rice will be mushy or soggy.

- Add diced carrots, red bell pepper, ground crayfish, stir and steam for 5-10 minutes then add shrimp, salt to taste if needed; steam for view minutes.

Serve with Dodo, Moin-Moin and any vegetable.
For Meat: Baked Chicken, Fried Chicken, Baked Fish, Fried Fish or Steak.
Serves 8 or more.

Fried Rice

There are many variations of fried rice, each with its own specific ingredients.

Ingredients
5 cups Rice
1 lb. Shrimp
1 cup cooked chicken gizzards – diced into tiny pieces
1 10oz. pkg. frozen peas & carrots
1 large onion - diced
Garlic - to taste (chopped)
4 maggi or knorr cubes - crushed
Thyme to taste
1 cup oil or butter
Water
Salt to taste

Directions
- Clean and boil gizzards with some salt until tender; cool then dice and set aside
- Drain water out of shrimp and peas/carrot vegetable. Set them aside.
- Add oil or butter into a deep cooking pot and heat over medium heat; add garlic and stir fry for one minute; add rice; stir fry (stir

continuously to avoid burning) for about 10 minutes or until rice is brown (not burn).

- Add seven (7) cups of water, maggi or knorr cubes, thyme, sliced onion, mix thoroughly, (add about ½ to one cup of water if needed); cover and steam for 20 to 30 minutes or until water is absorb completely into the rice. Do not add too much water or the rice will be mushy or soggy.
- Open and stir rice; add boiled gizzard; vegetable, stir and steam for another 10 minutes or until rice is cooked; add shrimp and steam for 5 minutes.
- Add salt to taste if needed.

Serve with: Dodo, Moin-Moin, Beans, and vegetable.
Meat: Baked Chicken, Fried Chicken, Baked Fish, Fried Fish or Steak.
Serves 8 or more.

Rice and Beans Porridge

Ingredient
2 cups Rice
1 lb. bag blackeye peas or African Red Beans
1 15oz. can of tomato sauce
3 tbsp. tomato paste
1 medium onion
2 habanera peppers (hot, adjust to taste)
1 red bell pepper
Garlic to taste
3 - 4 maggi or knorr cubes
½ -1 cup palm oil or 1/3 cup oil
Water
Salt to taste

Directions
- Blend tomato sauce, paste, onion, garlic, habanera peppers, and red bell pepper together. Add very little water as needed during blending for the blade to rotate. Set aside.
- Soak blackeye peas in cold water for about five minutes. (This will allow the beans to swell up and make it easy to remove the outer coat); or pour small amount of the beans into the blender, cover with water; grind for about 3 – 5 seconds (do not blend) and pour the beans into a large bowl; continue the process until finish.
- Cover beans with water; rub beans in between palms of both hands back and forth in the water to loosen the outer coat. The outer coat will naturally float to the top.
- Use a strainer to separate beans from the outer coat by draining the floating coats. Continue this process until beans is cleaned and no more coats or dark sport. Filter and change water as many times as needed.
- Pour cleaned bean into a deep cooking pot; cover with water and cook on medium high heat for 20 minutes to cook the bean half way done.
- Wash rice and rinse to remove excess starch; add to cooking beans; mix; cover and cook together for 15 – 20 minutes. Reduce heat if needed to prevent burning. Also you may need to add more water to the beans and rice if all the liquid is absorbed into the porridge while rice or beans is not done.
- Add tomato/pepper mixture, maggi or knorr cubes, thyme, curry, palm oil; stir, cover and steam for 15 minutes or until porridge is cooked at low heat to avoid burning. Also Stir porridge intermittently and continue simmering until done.
- Add salt if needed.

Serves 8 or more.

Rice and Chicken Casserole

<u>Ingredients</u>
1 cup uncooked rice
2 lbs. boneless chicken breast – remove skin and dice
1 10¾ oz. can condensed cream of mushroom
1 10¾ oz. can condensed cream of broccoli or celery
1 medium onion – dice
2 tablespoon olive oil or butter
2 14½ oz. can French style green beans rinse and drain
1 4oz. jar pimentos
1½ - 2 cup grated cheddar cheese
Salt to taste

<u>Directions</u>
Preheat oven to 350 degrees F.
- Clean and dice the chicken; per boil with some maggi for about five (5) minutes. (do not add water)
- Heat oil or butter in a frying pan over medium heat; add onion, pinch of salt, and sauté for five (5) minutes.
- Remove from heat and transfer to a large bowl; add all the remaining ingredients except cheese; stir all together thoroughly.
- Pour into a greased large casserole baking dish or pan; baked for 25-30 minutes or until bubbly;
- Add cheese and bake for 10 minutes.

Serves 4 or more

Rice and Goat Meat and Chicken Curry

<u>Ingredients</u>
1 lb. boneless goat meat - diced
1 lb. boneless chicken - diced
1 can 15 oz. diced tomatoes - on drained

1 medium onion - chopped

1 medium red bell pepper – chopped

1 medium green bell pepper – chopped

2 tablespoon curry powder – adjust to your taste

1 habanera pepper (optional)

1 cup chopped carrot

2 maggi cubes

Salt to taste

Water

6 - 8 cups of Cooked Rise

Directions

- Clean and boil goat meat and chicken with maggi cubes; add little water as most meat produces water as it cooks; drain excess broth.
- Combine meat/chicken, tomatoes, chopped onion, red and green bell peppers, carrot, habanera, curry powder one cup of water (add more if needed); stir and bring to a boil; reduce heat to low; cover and simmer for 45 minutes. Stir periodically.
- Add salt to taste and serve over hot cook rice.

Rice and Lemon Chicken

Ingredients

6 - 8 cups of Cooked Rise

4 chicken breast halves

8 pieces potatoes

1 red bell pepper - diced

1 red onion - chopped

3 4oz. can sliced mushrooms

2 lemons – divided

¼ cup olive oil

4 large garlic cloves – chopped

2-3 teaspoon dried oregano leaves

½ teaspoons coarsely ground black pepper

Salt to taste

Directions

- Using lemon zester, zest one lemon to measure 1½ tablespoons.
- Juice lemon to measure one tablespoon juice.
- In a mixing bowl, combine lemon zest, juice, oil, garlic, oregano, salt and black pepper; and mix well.
- Arrange chicken in a baking pan; brush chicken with a portion of the lemon juice mixture.
- Scrub potatoes well and pat dry and cut them in half; slice remaining lemon.
- In a mixing bowl, combine potatoes, bell pepper, onion, lemon slices and mushrooms with remaining lemon juice mixture; toss to mix.
- Arrange vegetables around chicken in the baking pan.
- Preheat oven to 400 degrees and bake chicken
- Bake for 30 minutes, then open and brush chicken and vegetables with the juice in the pan; continue baking for another 30 minutes or until chicken is done.
- Serve over rice.

Serves 2 - 4

Rice and Mushroom

Ingredients
5-6 cups Cooked Rice
2 8oz can slice mushroom
1 large onion – chopped
2 tablespoon olive oil
¼ lb. butter
3 tablespoon flour
2 cups milk
Salt and pepper

Pinch cayenne pepper

3 tablespoon chopped fresh parsley

½ cup dry bread crumbs

¼ cup grated Parmesan cheese

Directions

- In a large frying pan, sauté onion and mushrooms with three (3) tablespoons of butter for about 10 minutes; then add three (3) tablespoons butter and stir until melted.
- Stir in flour until smooth and lump free; gradually stir in milk; add some salt, ½ teaspoon pepper and cayenne.
- Bring to a boil and cook for three (3) minute; add rice and two (2) tablespoon parsley; mix and pour mixture into a 2-qt casserole pan; top with cheese and bake at 350 degrees.
- Serve with baked chicken, fish or steak.

Serves six.

Chapter 8

Rice-Complementing Recipes

Rice goes with everything. Everything goes with rice. In addition to the conventional rice recipes, there are those I call rice-complementing recipes. In many ethnic kitchens, certain items are served specifically to serve (pun intended) as accompaniments for rice. For example, in the Nigerian culinary preferences, there are options of "rice and dodo," "rice and moin-moin," "rice and beans," "rice and egg," and "rice and everything." The recipe collection here is just a sampling of the various food items that go well with rice. Try and experiment with the rice-complementing recipes below. Bon Appentit!

Fried Plantain (Dodo)

The Nigerian rice and dodo combination is a delightful favorite of mine.

Ingredients
6 pieces of ripe plantain
Salt to taste
Oil (any type) or palm oil

Instructions
- Slice or dice the plantain into pieces; add salt to taste.
- Pour palm oil or oil into a deep fryer or frying pan over medium high heat until hot.

- Place some cut plantain into the hot oil and fry until golden brown.
- Remove from the oil or palm oil and continue the process until finish.
- Drain on absorbent paper towel in the strainer.

Deji's Chicken Stove Top Stuffing Recipe

This is a very simple recipe I concocted for holiday celebrations. The product of this recipe can be used to stull roasted chicken or roasted duck.

Ingredients
1 pkg. (6 oz.) STOVE TOP Stuffing Mix for Chicken
1 stick of butter (or 3 table spoon full of margarine)
One fourth (1/4) cup of cooked white rice (long grain)

Instructions
On the stove, bring 3 cups of water to boil in large pot.
Add the butter or margarine to the boiling water until it melts.
Reduce heat to low.
Add stove top and mix constantly.
Note: If there is too much water, the stove will turn too mushy, soggy, or runny.

If this happens, add more stove top dressing.

The mix should have the consistency similar to thick oat meal.

Add the cooked white rice. The rice should blend in and be unnoticeable in the mix. If there is too much rice, the mixture will be too thick. The idea is to have the rice provide something like rice milk. Not too much or too little.

Turn off heat.

Cover the pot and leave on stove for about 15 minutes before serving.

This recipe requires experimentation to discover each chef's preference. Make adjustments to suit your needs. You may embellish it with your own ingredients and substitutes.

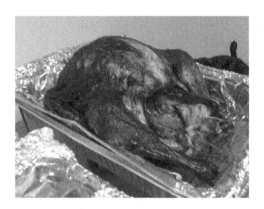 

Nigerian Water-Yam Fritters (Ọjọjọ)

<u>Ingredients</u>
1 large African water-yam - Peel skin and grate
1 red bell pepper - chopped
1 medium onion - chopped
1-2 hot chili pepper - chopped (hot, adjust to taste)
2 -3 maggi or knorr cubes - crushed

Oil or African palm oil - to fry
Salt to taste

<u>Directions</u>
- Peel the skin off the water-yam and grate into a mixing bowl.
- Add chopped red bell pepper, onion, pepper, crushed maggi or knorr, and salt to taste.
- Mix thoroughly.

Frying:

- Deep-fry the mixture by scooping a little amount individually into hot oil and fry until golden. Scoop as many as the frying pan will take. Continue the process until finish.
- Drain on absorbent paper towel in a strainer to remove excess oil.
- Serve hot.

Serves many.

Dad's Peanut Butter Fudge (original by Virgil Spainhower) (Provided by Penny Davis)

<u>Ingredients</u>
½ c crisco
4 c sugar
1 can of evaporated milk
1 c peanut butter
2 c marshmallow fluff

<u>Directions</u>
Mix first 3 ingredients, cook until reaches soft ball consistency. Remove from heat, add peanut butter and marshmallow fluff. Mix thoroughly and pour into greased pan, set for 2 hours to harden. Enjoy!

No-Bake Cookies
(Provided by Penny Davis)

Special cookies are good as desserts after a meal of rice.

<u>Ingredients</u>
4 c sugar
1 c milk
2 sticks of butter
1 c cocoa
2 c peanut butter
2 tsp vanilla
6 c oatmeal

<u>Directions</u>
Cook first 4 ingredients over low heat, bring to boil for a couple of minutes. Remove from heat, add peanut butter, vanilla and oatmeal. Drop on wax paper and let sit for a couple of hours.

Nigerian Moin-Moin (Steamed Beans Cake)

<u>Ingredients</u>
1 lb. bag Blackeye Peas or African Red Beans
1 medium red bell pepper
1 medium onion
4 pieces dry fish (shredded) or one can corned beef
3 - 4 crayfish maggi cubes – crushed
3 - 4 cups of water
½ cup palm oil or canola oil – warm
Salt to taste

<u>Directions</u>
Step 1
• Clean Blackeye Peas or African Red Beans as follows:

- Soak blackeye peas in cold water for about five minutes. (This will allow the beans to swell up and make it easy to remove the outer coat); or pour small amount of the beans into the blender, cover with water; grind for about 3 – 5 seconds (do not blend) and pour the beans into a large bowl; continue the process until finish.
- Cover beans with water; rub beans in-between palms of both hands back and forth in the water to lose the outer coat. The outer coat will naturally float to the top.
- Use a strainer to separate beans from the outer coat by draining the floating coats. Continue this process until beans is cleaned and no more coats or dark sport. Filter and change water as many times as needed.

- Blending Step
- Combine cleaned beans, bell pepper, and onion and blend until mixture becomes a smooth paste. Add water as needed for the blender to rotate. However, do not add too much or beans will become watery. The beans batter (paste) should be a little thinner than Pancake batter.

Step 2

- Make pouches/pockets with aluminum foil or use individual non-stick cupcake cups.
- Shred dry fish and clean in hot water.
- Warm palm oil or oil.
- Pour blended beans into a mixing bowl and mix with a wooden spoon very well to aerate it; add shredded fish or corned beef, crushed maggi cubes and mix; add warm palm oil; salt if needed and mix thoroughly until lump free.
- The beans batter should be a little bite thinner than cake batter.
- Scoop the blended beans into the aluminum pouches one by one; fill half-way to allow room for expansion during cooking. Seal the foil at the top by folding several times.

- Arrange moin-moin into a deep cooking pot and add about 3 - 4 cups of water. Add more if needed.
- Cook for 30 - 45 minutes at medium high.
- Moin-moin is done when it is firm to the touch after exposure to the air for few minutes.
- Unwrap, slice and serve.

Serve with rice for 8 or more.

Puff-Puff (Nigerian Donuts)

<u>Ingredients</u>
½ bag 5 lbs. All-purpose flour
2 cups of sugar or adjust to taste
2 sachets quick-rising yeast
1 tsp. salt
7-8 cups of very warm water

<u>Directions</u>
- In a large bowl, combine flour, sugar, yeast, salt and mix.

- Add very warm water slowly and mix until desire softness or thickness and lumps free with hand.
- Cover mixed batter and set aside to rise for about three to four hours in a warm or hot spot in the house or outside in the sun. Batter can be mixed and set aside to rise over night also.

Frying:

- Add oil into a deep fryer and heat. Test the oil by dropping a little batter into the hot oil; batter should float to the top.
- Use a scooper, 1/8 of a cup size, or 1/4 of a cup size to scoop up the batter and gently drop into the hot oil to form a ball.
- Also batter can be scooped up by forming a scoop with your hand and scoop up the batter and gently drop into the hot oil. Please be careful with this method.
- Deep fry until light brown or golden brown.
- Continue this process until the batter is finished.
- Optional: Sprinkle puff-puff with powdered sugar.

Serve hot. Okay to warm in the microwave oven.
Serves 25 and up

Nigerian Pepper Stew

Rice goes well with hot spicy stew. This Nigerian stew is a unique blend of tomatoes, onion, fresh hot red pepper, ginger, garlic, seasoning and oil or palm oil.

<u>Ingredients</u>
2 lbs. assorted meat – cube (See list & cooking direction at the end of the chapter)
2 15¼ oz. can tomato sauce
1 6oz. can tomato paste
1 large onion
Fresh Ginger – to your taste
Fresh Garlic – to your taste
3 habanera peppers (hot, adjust to taste)
2 red bell peppers
4 maggi or knorr cubes
½ cup oil – less if prefer
Water
Salt to taste

<u>Directions</u>
• Blend tomato sauce, paste, onion, ginger, garlic, habanera peppers and red bell peppers together; add water as needed for the blender to rotate and blend until smooth). Set aside.
• Boil assorted meat: See list & cooking direction at the end of the chapter.
• In a deep cooking pot, combine blended tomato/pepper mixture; maggi or knorr and cook for 20 minutes. Stir occasionally during cooking to avoid burning the sauce. Add ½ to one cup of water if mixture appears too thick and cook for five (5) minutes.
• Add cooked assorted meat; stir and cook for 15 minutes.
• Add oil, cover and cook at low to medium heat for 15 – 20 minutes. Stir occasionally during cooking to allow ingredients to mix evenly.
• Add salt to taste as needed.

Serve over rice.

Note: If cooking fish, do not boil the fish; clean and cut into pieces, sprinkle with little salt and set aside for 30 minutes to marinate before cooking. Instead of stirring soup, lift the pot and shake the pot to mix the contents. This will avoid getting the fish crumpled.

Nigerian Fried Pepper Stew without Meat

Instructions
2 15¼oz. can tomato sauce
1 6oz. can tomato paste
1 large onion
Fresh Ginger – to your taste
Fresh Garlic – to your taste
3 habanera peppers (hot, adjust to taste)
2 red bell peppers
4 maggi or knorr cubes
Curry powder to taste
Ground thyme to taste
2-3 cups of Oil or more
Salt to taste

Directions

If adding fish to the Fried Stew:
• Clean and cut fresh fish into cubes; season with salt and set aside in a strainer for about 20-30 minutes for the water to drain and marinate then fry and Set aside.

If adding meat to the Fried Stew:
• Cut into pieces boil with any meat seasoning until tender. Add little water as most meat produces water as it cooks. Remove from

the pot and put in a strainer to drain any juice from the meat then fry and set aside.

- Blend tomato sauce, paste, onion, ginger, garlic, habanera peppers, and red bell peppers together; add very little water during blending but enough for the blade to rotate.
- In a deep cooking pot, add mixture of blended tomato/pepper, maggi or knorr, thyme and curry. Cover and cook for 30 - 45 minutes at mid heat or until fairly reduced to thick paste; stir occasionally during cooking to prevent burning; reduce heat if necessary.
- Add leftover oil from frying the meat or fish; stir and cook for another 10 minutes. The oil will float to the top. However, if oil is not floating on top, continue cooking at a low heat on cover so that the sauce will become condense lowly and the oil will float to the top. Fried stew takes a lot of oil! So add more if needed.

- Add fried meat, snail or fried fish and stir. At a low heat, simmer for another 10 - 15 minutes.
- Add salt if needed to taste.

Serve over rice, beans or any of the soups in this book.

Seafood Soup

<u>Ingredients</u>
1 pound shrimp
4 - 5 pieces crabs – cut into 2 each
1 large onion – chopped
2 clove garlic – chopped
1 large green bell pepper – chopped
2 28-oz. can tomato
1 16-oz. can tomato sauce
1 cup red wine

1 bay leaf
1 teaspoon basil
½ teaspoon oregano leaves
¼ cup olive oil

<u>Directions</u>
- Clean and boil crabs; set aside.
- In a frying pan or saucepan, sauté onion, garlic and green bell pepper in olive oil.
- Add tomato, tomato sauce, wine, bay leaf, basil and oregano; stir well and bring to boil; reduce heat and simmer for 20 minutes.
- Add crab and shrimp; cover and simmer ten (10) minutes; remove bay leaf and discard
- Serve hot over rice.

Note: This soup can also be prepared with fresh fish, for example fresh Tilapia.

John Colombi's "Death by 4 Cheese and 3 Meat" Lasagna

Surprisingly, rice goes okay with lasagna just as lasagna goes with rice. Be bold. Experiment with new tastes. So, I am presenting the recipe contribution of my AFIT colleague, Dr. John M. Colombi. This makes two 13 ½in x 9 ½in x 4 inch deep pans…. Always nice to have an extra one to share or freeze for later. Strongly recommend using a deep 4 inch pan to be able to build enough layers and it also prevents bubbling over in the oven. This recipe is at least 3 ½ inches tall!

<u>Component Ingredients and Instructions</u>

Ricotta Cheese Filling: Combine and set aside
2 2lb containers Ricotta
2 Tbsp parsley

½-1 tsp oregano
4-5 eggs beaten

Meat Filling:
Brown, drain and set aside
1 lb mild Italian sausage (remove casing)
1 lb hot Italian sausage (remove casing)
2 lbs lean ground beef
1 small onion finely chopped, cooked with the ground beef

Sauce:
Simmer while preparing the other ingredients
28oz tomato sauce (any kind)
½ -1 green pepper chopped
½-1 tsp garlic power or fresh (2-3 cloves minced)
Salt, pepper to taste …other great additions are basil, onion or oregano

Cheeses:
Grated, fine to medium, and set aside
½ - ¾ lb Romano
½ - ¾ lb Parmesan
12-16oz Shredded Mozzarella (pizza cheese)

Lasagna Noodles:
Add noodles to boiling water, with a little olive oil, and cook for 8-10 minutes.
Don't overcook. Cool the partially cooked noodles in ice water, then spread the cooked noodles on waxed paper (sprayed with cooking spray) until you are ready to begin building the lasagna stack.

The Grand Instructions
Now the fun begins. Do the stacking!

1. Cover bottom of pan (about 1½ cups of sauce).
2. Layer of lasagna noodles (3 strips)

3. Spread about ¼ of the Ricotta Cheese Filling (sprinkle on some Romano and Parmesan) – I would guess 2-3 cups of cheese filling per layer
4. Layer of lasagna noodles (3 strips)
5. Spread about ¼ of the ground beef and sausage (pour on about 1 ½-2 cups of sauce, then sprinkle on some Romano and Parmesan)
6. Repeat steps 2, 3, 4,5
7. Last (top) layer of lasagna noodles (3 or 4 strips)
8. Gentle flatten the top of the lasagna. Presentation, like taste, is also important
9. Pour on about 1 ½-2 cups of sauce, then sprinkle on some Romano and Parmesan, then cover completely with 12-16oz Mozzarella cheese.

Preheat oven to 350°. Cover with aluminum foil. Try to make a slight tent so the foil doesn't bake into the top cheese. Bake for 30-40 minutes. If you plan on eating right away, remove aluminum foil and brown for 10-15 minutes more. Please be reminded that the internal temperature for safe eating should be 165°. Serve. You can also freeze the baked lasagna for up to a week... simply reheat. Many people prefer reheated lasagna since it will be more firm and comes out as perfect squares. Either way - Enjoy!

<u>My Note</u>: You can guess by the structural complexity of this recipe that Dr. John Colombi is an engineer, a systems engineer to be more specific. Yes, a systems configuration comes out clearly in the articulation of the formulation of the recipe.

Suya for Rice

Suya is a meat-based grilled Nigerian snack. I love pieces of delicious Suya on my steamed white rice sans stew. Try it. Your palate will appreciate your bold spirit. Suya is normally spicy hot, but you can temper it down to your mild taste.

Ingredients

3 tbsp finely-ground roast peanuts, shelled and de-skinned
1 tsp cayenne pepper
1 tsp paprika
1 tsp salt
1/2 tsp ground ginger
1/2 tsp garlic powder
1/2 tsp onion powder
500g meat (beef, chicken, lamb, etc.) cut into bite-sized cubes
1 onion, peeled and cut into chunks
tomato, cut into chunks
red bell pepper de-seeded and cut into chunks

Instructions

Stir the spices into the peanut powder, mixing well then divide the mix into two bowls, equal amounts in both. Set one bowl aside.

Dip and roll the meat in the contents of one bowl, making sure that the meat is completely coated. Allow the meat to marinate in this mix for at least half an hour then place the meat on skewers, alternating with onion, tomato and bell pepper. Cook under a grill or on a barbecue and sprinkle with the reserved peanut mix.

Gumbo

(provided by Penny Davis)

Gumbo on rice or rice on Gumbo, whichever comes first, is my favorite food, but then any rice-based dish is my favorite. Thank you, Penny!

1 chicken
1 bag of shrimp
1 pkg of sweet basil brats (sliced and cooked)
1 lb bag of frozen okra

1/2 cup plus 2 Tbls cooking oil

1/2 cup flour

2 cups chopped onions

1 cup chopped green pepper

1/2 cup chopped celery

1 16oz can chopped tomatoes

1 bay leaf

1 tsp thyme

1 tsp basil

1 tsp gumbo file powder (seasoning you can find at Walmart)

1/2 tsp sage

1/2 tsp black/white pepper

1/4 tsp cayenne pepper

2 tsp salt

Boil chicken until done--pour off stock and set aside. Allow chicken to cool, remove from bones and set aside. In a large heavy skillet saute the okra in oil (2 tbls) for about 10/15 minutes or until the "ropiness" is gone. Set aside. In a large dutch oven, heat 1/2 cup oil over medium heat, add the flour and make a dark roux--cook the oil/flour until it is a color of peanut butter, keep stirring/scraping the bottom of the pan. Once the right color is achieved, add the onion, pepper, celery and saute until tender. During this process allow the veggies to stick to the bottom of the pan, then scrape with a wooden spoon--this allows some of the natural sugars in the onions to carmelize and adds depth to the flavor! When the veggies are tender, add the tomatoes, sausage and sauteed okra. Cook for about 15 minutes. Add the bay leaf, thyme, basil, sage, peppers and salt and mix well. Pour in about 8 cups of the chicken stock, then simmer for 1 hour. Then add the chicken and shrimp, simmer another 15 minutes then serve over steamed rice.

Shrimp Etouffee
(provided by Penny Davis)

1/2 cup butter
1/4 cup flour
3 cups chopped onion
1/2 cup celery
1/2 chopped green pepper
2 tsp minced garlic
1/2 tsp basil
1/2 tsp black/white pepper
1/4 tsp cayenne pepper
1 tsp salt
1 tsp paprika
1/2 tsp tabasco sauce
1 1/2 shrimp or chicken stock
1 lb peeled shrimp
1/2 cup thinly sliced green onions
1 Tbls chopped parsley

In large Dutch oven over a medium heat, melt butter, add flour and make roux the color of peanut butter, add onions, celery, pepper. Cook veggies until translucent and tender. Add the garlic, basil, peppers, salt, paprika, cook for 2 minutes. Stir in tabasco sauce and stock and bring to a gentle boil. Add shrimp, green onions, and parsley. Simmer for another 5/10 min then serve over steamed rice!

Chapter 9

World Trade, Economics, and Politics of Rice

The impact of rice on political wrangling was demonstrated in the Nigerian 2015 presidential general democratic election when the previous administration was accused of allocating bags of rice to selected parts of the country as a way to sway votes in favor of the incumbent government. The scam came to light after it was revealed by the supposed recipients that the bags of rice were never released to the intended recipients. Indeed, rice has become the bane of politics in some parts of the world.

A June 18, 2014 online posting by Thelma Dumpit-Murillo (http:// www.manilatimes.net/the-politics-of-rice/105165/; accessed January 24, 2016)) provides a good account of the *politics of rice* around the world. She opined that politics and social factors are very connected with the rice industry. As I mentioned earlier in this book, rice is a world-wide-consumed commodity. So, a whole lot of people are affected by rice politics around the world. Many organizations have focused on regulating and promoting the trade of rice. The International Rice Commission was created in 1949 to supervise the production, distribution, consumption, and conservation of rice. In 1994, the World Trade Organization created an Agreement on Agriculture which called for reduced government intervention and trade liberalization of rice on the world market, but it turns out that European Union, Japan, and the United States are still protecting their rice producers and subsidizing their exports. This has an adverse impact on other rice-producing countries, particularly in developing countries, which have followed the world rice trade guidelines and reduced their subsidies, which in turn increased their domestic cost of rice production. Since the prices of rice are falling around the world, it becomes difficult for rice producers in developing countries to be competitive on the world market.

In 2004, the United Nations declared that it was the official year of rice. The UN wanted to raise awareness of the political, economics, and social issues associated with rice. There is even an official site for the International Year of Rice at http://www.fao.org/rice2004/. Just as the rice trade has many social and political issues, it also has many environmental issues. Researchers around the world are studying the effects that producing rice has on the environment and ecosystems. More needs to be done in studying and advancing the role of rice in global political systems. All rice lovers should be aware of the behind-the-scene political, trade, and economic issues affecting their favorite food. According to World Trade sources, as of 2014, the top 10 rice-exporting countries (by dollar value) are listed below.

1. India: US$7.9 billion (31.8% of total rice exports)
2. Thailand: $5.4 billion (21.9%)
3. Pakistan: $2.2 billion (8.8%)
4. United States: $2 billion (8%)
5. Vietnam: $1.8 billion (7.4%)
6. Italy: $699.5 million (2.8%)
7. Uruguay: $513.1 million (2.1%)
8. Brazil: $397 million (1.6%)
9. China: $378.3 million (1.5%)
10. Australia: $352.8 million (1.4%)

It is expected that the above export shares would have changed by now due to the continual dynamism of the world rice market. Also, the statistics here are on dollar values of exports. The statistics on metric tonnage of exports will show a slighted different rank order.

Price differentials due to tariffs and subsidies affect rank-ordering based on dollar value compared to metric tonnage.

Long live our beloved rice!

Chapter 10

Useful Kitchen References

Uses of Vinegar

➤ A mixture of salt and vinegar will clean coffee and tea stains from chinaware.

➤ Freshen vegetables. Soak wilted vegetables in 2 cups of water and a tablespoon of vinegar.

➤ Boil better eggs by adding 2 tablespoons to water before boiling. Keeps them from cracking.

➤ Marinating meat in vinegar kills bacteria and tenderizes the meat. Use one-quarter cup vinegar for a two to three pound roast, marinate overnight, and then cook without draining or rinsing the meat.

➤ Add herbs to the vinegar when marinating as desired.

➤ Put vinegar on a cloth and let sit on the back of your kitchen faucet and it removes hard water stains.

➤ Vinegar can help to dissolve mineral deposits that collect in automatic drip coffee makers. Fill the reservoir with vinegar and run it through a brewing cycle. Rinse thoroughly with water when the cycle is finished. (Be sure to check the owner's manual for specific instructions).

➤ Brass, copper and pewter will shine if cleaned with the following mixture. Dissolve 1 teaspoon of salt in one (1) cup of distilled vinegar.

- Clean the dishwasher by running a cup of vinegar through the whole cycle once a month to reduce soap build up on the inner mechanisms and on glassware.
- Deodorize the kitchen drain. Pour a cup of vinegar down the drain once a week. Let stand 30 minutes and then flush with cold water.
- Unclog a drain. Pour a handful of baking soda down the drain and add ½ cup of vinegar. Rinse with hot water.
- Eliminate onion odor by rubbing vinegar on your fingers before and after slicing.
- Clean and disinfect wood cutting boards by wiping with full strength vinegar.
- Cut grease and odor on dishes by adding a tablespoon of vinegar to hot soapy water.
- Clean a teapot by boiling a mixture of water and vinegar in it. Wipe away the grime.
- Clean and deodorize the garbage disposal by making vinegar ice cubes and feed them down the disposal. After grinding, run cold water through.
- Clean and deodorize jars. Rinse mayonnaise, peanut butter, and mustard jars with vinegar when empty.
- Get rid of cooking smells by letting a small pot of vinegar and water simmer on the stove.
- Clean the refrigerator by washing with a solution of equal parts water and vinegar.
- Clean stainless steel by wiping with vinegar dampened cloth.
- Clean china and fine glassware by adding a cup of vinegar to a sink of warm water. Gently dip the glass or china in the solution and let dry.
- Get stains out of pots by filling the pots with a solution of three (3) tablespoons of vinegar to a pint of water. Boil until stain loosens and can be washed away.
- Clean food-stained pots and pans by filling the pots and pans with vinegar and let stand for thirty minutes. Then rinse in hot, soapy water.

➤ Clean the microwave by boiling a solution of ¼ cup of vinegar and 1 cup of water in the microwave. It will loosen splattered on food and deodorize.

➤ Make buttermilk. Add a tablespoon of vinegar to a cup of milk and let it stand for five (5) minutes to thicken.

➤ Replace a lemon by substituting ¼ teaspoon of vinegar for 1 teaspoon of lemon juice.

➤ Firm up gelatin by adding a teaspoon of vinegar for every box of gelatin used. To keep those molded desserts from sagging in the summer heat.

➤ Prepare fluffier rice by adding a teaspoon of vinegar to the water when it boils.

➤ Make wine vinegar by mixing two (2) tablespoons of vinegar with 1 teaspoon of dry red wine.

➤ Debug fresh vegetables by washing them in water with vinegar and salt. Bugs float off.

➤ Scale fish more easily by rubbing with vinegar five (5) minutes before scaling.

➤ Prevent soap film on glassware by placing a cup of vinegar on the bottom rack of your dishwasher, run for five minutes, then run though the full cycle.

➤ The minerals found in foods and water will often leave a dark stain on aluminum utensils. This stain can be easily removed by boiling a solution of 1 tablespoon of distilled vinegar per cup of water in the utensil. Utensils may also be boiled in the solution.

➤ Unsightly film in small-necked bottles and other containers can be cleaned by pouring vinegar into the bottle and shaking. For tougher stains, add a few tablespoons of rice or sand and shake vigorously. Rinse thoroughly and repeat until clean or determined hopeless.

➤ After cleaning the bread box, keep it smelling sweet by wiping it down with a cloth moistened in distilled vinegar.

➤ To eliminate fruit stains from your hands, rub your hands with a little distilled vinegar and wipe with a cloth

> Grease build-up in an oven can be prevented by wiping with a cleaning ran that has been moistened in distilled vinegar and water.
> Formica tops and counters will shine in cleaned with a cloth soaked in distilled vinegar.
> No-wax linoleum will shine better if wiped with a solution of ½ cup of white vinegar in ½ gallon of water.
> Stains on hard-to-clean glass, aluminum, or porcelain utensils may be loosened by boiling in a solution of one part vinegar to eight parts water. The utensils should then be washed in hot soapy water.
> A mixture of one part vinegar to two parts water will defrost car windshield easily in Winter.
> On the personal health side, vinegar will calm upset stomach, relieve coughs, mitigate nausea, reduce hiccups, cool sunburn, alleviate sore throat, relieve itchy skin, soothe bladder infection, treat burns, aid digestion, and bar infection

Uses of Ginger

> Ginger up! Ginger can spice up a lot of things with ginger. Ginger is a multi-faceted root not only for cooking, but also for therapeutic applications in the home. Two common applications are for cough/sore throat therapy and relief of indigestion.
> Directions: Scrape off the bark from the root, and cut the remaining root into small, cough-drop-sized pieces. The taste is very strong, and has a spicy flavor. For mild relief, suck the ginger for a light dose of the juice, and for more intensity, bite slightly into the root to squeeze more of the juice out. This is very effective if you feel you are about to cough.
> Ginger also acts as a digestive aid. It can cut through excess mucous, and help relieve an upset stomach. Chew up on the cough-drop ginger pieces and swallow them to relieve

indigestion. There is a ginger tea that helps with this, with colds, and with coughing.

➤ Making Ginger Tea: To make ginger tea, prepare the root the same way it is done for cough drops. Cut the ginger into chunks, and put in a saucepan with a good quantity of filtered or spring water. Slowly cook the brew until about three quarters of the water boils off. This will produce a very spicy tea, which will aid the digestion and even help strengthen the immune system.

Uses of Baking Soda

Baking soda is a chemical compound, bicarbonate of soda, that appears as a fine powder. It releases bubbles of carbon dioxide when it interacts with an acid and a liquid. It is most commonly used in baking, where it acts as a leavening agent. It has many different uses in the kitchen. It often works better than many commercially available and expensive products for the same uses.

- Sprinkle baking soda on grease or electrical fire to safely put it out. This also works for car engine fire. Baking soda will also put out fires in clothing, fuel, wood, upholstery and rugs.
- Clean vegetables and fruit with baking soda. Sprinkle in water, soak and rinse the vegetables.
- Wash garbage cans with baking soda to freshen and eliminate odors.
- Oil and grease in clothes stains will wash out better with soda added to the washing water.
- Clean fridge and freezer with dry baking soda sprinkled on a damp cloth and rinse with clear water.
- Deodorize fridge and freezer by putting in an open container of baking soda to absorb odors. Stir and turn over the soda from time to time. Replace every 2 months.
- Wash food and drink containers with baking soda and water.

- Wash marble-topped kitchen cabinet furniture with a solution of three tablespoons of baking soda in one quart of warm water. Let stand awhile and then rinse with clear water.
- Wash out thermos bottles and cooling containers with soda and water to get rid of stale smells.
- To remove stubborn stains from marble or plastic surfaces, scour with a paste of soda and water.
- Wash glass or stainless steel coffee pots (but not aluminum) in a soda solution (three teaspoons of soda to one quart water).
- For better cleaning of coffee maker, run it through its cycle with baking soda solution and rinse clean.
- Give baby bottles a good cleaning with soda and hot water.
- Sprinkle soda on barbecue grills, let soak, and then rinse off.
- Polish silverware with dry soda on a damp cloth. Rub, rinse, and dry.
- Reduce odor build-up in dishwasher by sprinkling some baking soda on the bottom.
- Run dishwasher through its cycle with baking soda in it instead of soap to give it a good cleaning.
- To remove burned-on food from a pan, let the pan soak in baking soda and water for ten minutes before washing. Alternately, scrub the pot with dry baking soda and a moist scouring pad.
- For a badly-burned pan with a thick layer of burned-on food, pour a thick layer of baking soda directly onto the bottom of the pan. Then sprinkle on just enough water so as to moisten the soda. Leave the pot overnight. Scrub it clean next day.
- Rub stainless steel and chrome with a moist cloth and dry baking soda to shine it up. Rinse and dry. On stainless steel, scrub in the Directions of the grain.
- Clean plastic, porcelain and glass with dry baking soda on a damp cloth. Rinse and dry.
- Keep drains clean and free-flowing by putting four tablespoons of soda in them each week. Flush the soda down with hot water.
- To remove strong odors from hands, wet hands and rub them hard with baking soda, then rinse.

- Sprinkle baking soda on wet toothbrush and brush teeth and dentures with it.
- Apply soda directly to insect bites, rashes, and poison ivy to relieve discomfort. Make a paste with water.
- For plucking chickens, add one teaspoon of baking soda to the boiling water. The feathers will come off easier and flesh will be clean and white.
- Add to water to soak dried beans to make them more digestible.

Use to remove melted plastic bread wrapper from toaster, dampen cloth and make a mild abrasive with baking soda.

Uses of Lemon Juice

"A little lemon juice makes everything taste better."
- Virginia Sanborn Burleigh

Lemons originated in India and have been used for trading purposes for centuries. Lemons were originally called "the golden apples." This inexpensive fruit is very useful and versatile.

- To make substitute buttermilk, mix one cup of milk with a tablespoon of lemon juice for a buttermilk substitute that works great!

- To sanitize dishwasher and remove mineral deposits and odors, remove all dishes. Place 1/4 cup of lemon juice in the soap dispenser and run through the normal cycle. Dishwasher will be clean and smell wonderful!

- To clean copper pots, cover the surface of a half lemon with salt and scrub. Rinse and buff with a soft cloth for a beautiful shine.

- To clean silver, clean with lemon juice and buff with a soft cloth.

- Lemon juice also cleans the tarnish off brass.

- To remove the smell of garlic or onions from hands, rub with a lemon slice and rinse.

Uses of Honey

Honey is the only food in the world that will not spoil or rot. It will do what some people refer to as "turning to sugar." In reality honey is always honey. However, when left in a cool dark place for a long time it will crystallize.

"You can sweeten two pots with only one drop of honey."
-                    Deji Badiru, June 22, 2010

"You catch more flies with honey than with vinegar." – A Common Saying

Both honey and vinegar have their respective uses in the kitchen. For honey's sake, we list the following kitchen uses:

- Tasty additive to foods and drinks
- Use as a sugar substitute when cooking or baking
- Remedy for diabetic ulcer to speed up the healing process
- Relaxant for anxiety and nervousness
- Antibacterial solution --- Honey has antibacterial properties due to its acidic nature and produces hydrogen peroxide through an enzymic process
- Remedy for burns, particularly as first-aid in kitchen accidents
- Treatment for sore throat --- to grease the passage of food on the gastronomic journey
- Enhancement to Vitamin A
- Immune system and energy booster
- Antiseptic

- Honey taken with cinnamon powder can ease stomachache
- Good antioxidant

When honey jar lid hardens, loosen the lid by boiling some water and sitting the honey Jar in the hot water. Turn off the heat and let the jar content liquefy. It is then as good as before. Never boil honey or put it in a microwave. To do so will kill the enzymes in the honey.

Facts on Honey and Cinnamon

- It is found that a mixture of honey and Cinnamon cures most diseases.
- Honey is produced in most of the countries of the world.
- Honey can be used without any side effects for any kind of diseases.
- Even though honey is sweet, if taken in the right dosage as a medicine, it does not harm diabetic patients.
- For bladder infection, take two tablespoons of cinnamon powder and one teaspoon of honey in a glass of lukewarm water and drink it. It destroys the germs in the bladder.
- For upset stomach, honey taken with cinnamon powder mitigates stomach ache and also reduces the symptoms of stomach ulcers.
- Some studies done in India and Japan conjecture that if honey is taken with cinnamon powder, the stomach is relieved of gas.
- It is believed that cinnamon powder sprinkled on two tablespoons of honey, taken before meal, can relieve acidity to facilitate digestion.

About the author

Deji Badiru is an award-winning author, educator, researcher, and administrator. He is a member of several professional organizations and author of several books and technical journal articles. He has served as a consultant to several organizations around the world and has received awards for his teaching, writing, leadership, and managerial accomplishments. Badiru has diverse areas of avocation. His professional accomplishments are coupled with his passion of writing about everyday events, interpersonal issues, social responsibilities, livelihood, and lifestyles.

Printed in the United States
By Bookmasters